Back of the Pond

Mercedes Benoit-Penney

Back of the Pond

Copyright © 2018 by Mercedes Benoit-Penney, St. Clair Publications

All rights reserved. No part of this publication may be reproduced or transmitted in any form or by any means, electronic or mechanical, including photocopying, recording, or by any information storage and retrieval system, without written permission from the author.

Author Disclaimer: To the best of my knowledge, all historical entries in this book are factual; all characters are real, with a few exceptions where humor only was intended; and all events were relayed as my memory allowed.

ISBN 978-1-947514-02-7

Printed in the United States of America by

St. Clair Publications

PO Box 726

McMinnville, TN   37111-0726

http://stclairpublications.com/

The inside cover image is a 1928 painting of the Indian Head Range by Austin White (son of Thomas LeBlanc and Julianna LeBlanc). At the age of seventeen, Austin painted Indian Head as he viewed it from his father's fence. In later years, the last knob to the far right of the painting was blasted to provide a breakwater for the harbor channel.

Table of Contents

Dedication 1

A Life Remembered 2

In Memory Of 4

Preface 7

Introduction: History of Stephenville.. 8

Chapter 1: Recollection of 50s and 60s 9

Chapter 2: Mona 33

Chapter 3: Margie 40

Chapter 4: Those Trying School Days.. 44

Chapter 5: And Why French, Oh Lord! 52

Chapter 6: The Friendly Invasion 59

Chapter 7: Life's Challenges 80

Chapter 8: Allderdice Syndrome 92

Chapter 9: Disregard For French and Mi'kmaq Culture 101

Chapter 10: Lamente de Mon Père 110

Chapter 11: Paradise Lost.. 121

Acknowledgments 307

Bibliography 309

About the Author 319

Notes.. 320

Dedication

<u>Back of the Pond</u> is dedicated to my husband Bill, for all the patience he showed while I wrote this book, and to my three children, Bobby, Dawn (Kent Burton) and Laura (Jonathan Flaven), as well as their amazing families.

L – R: Jonah, Lucas Flaven
Grandchildren

L – R: Landen, Ashlyn, Hudson Burton,
Grandchildren

Love always,
Nanny Penney

A Life Remembered

If I had to name a catalyst for the writing of this book, it would have to be my mom.

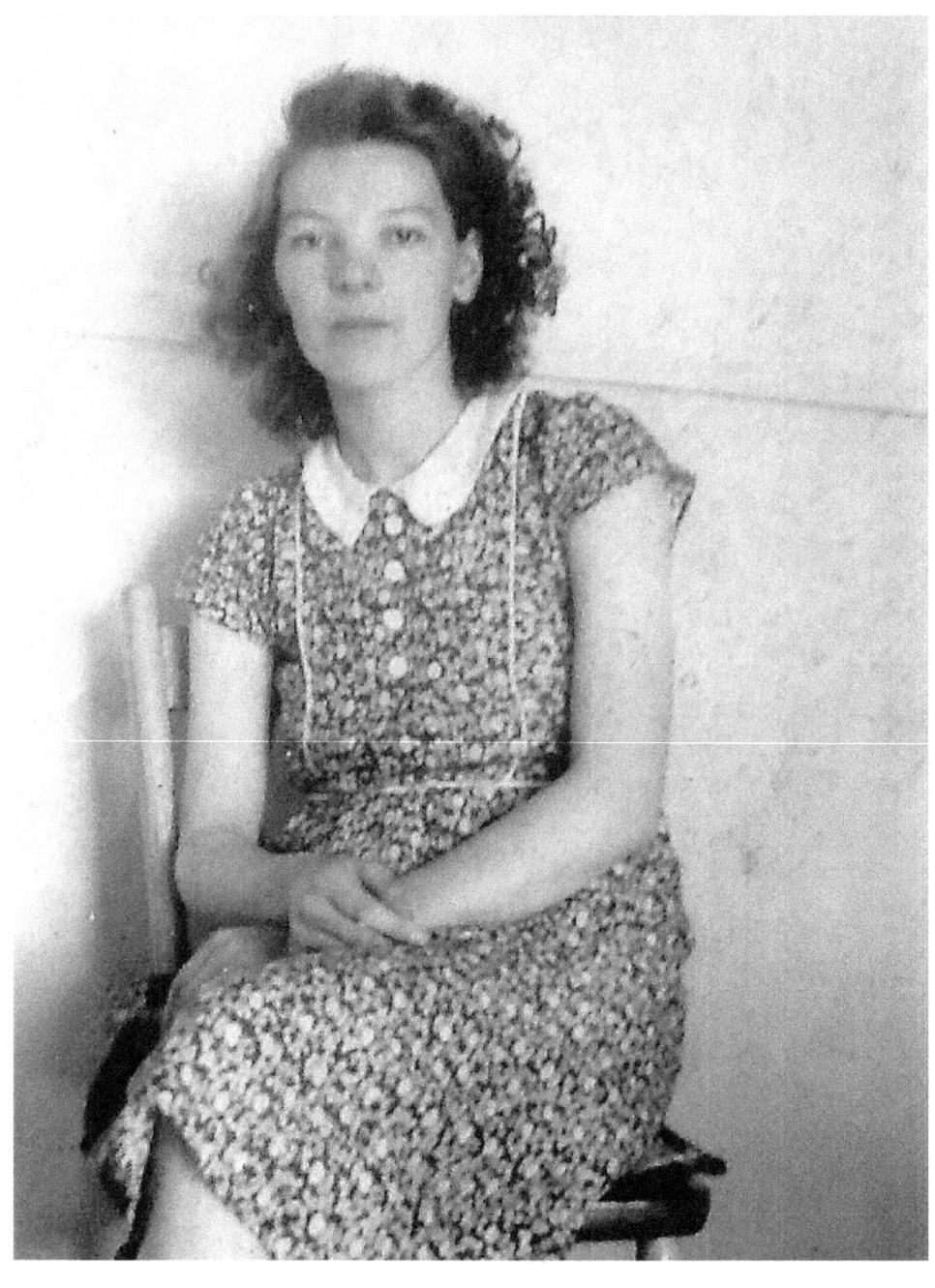

Agnita LeBlanc

BACK OF THE POND

In reflecting on the past, I longed for more of her in my life. I remember, as we grew up in the lane, on what is now called James Street (after my grandfather, James Benoit), how our family of 10 was so blessed, not to have lost any siblings, as the years went by. All around us, though, young children died, for a variety of reasons. My cousin Mona, age 9, was one example, but there were many more.

In retrospect, when I scribbled for therapeutic reasons, or to pass the time, my mind would always draw me back to when I was a child, to a time before mom's death, before I turned 21. The more I wrote and researched, the more I filled a void that was left after my mother passed away, from a very painful battle with cancer, in 1972. I learned about her childhood and what made her who she was. I learned about her numerous struggles, both mental and physical; the many obstacles to her identity, and how she must have felt when her French name was taken from her and replaced by the anglicized version — White. I learned of the struggle that she and others faced when their French language was taken from them and replaced with English; how the school system at that time punished them if they uttered a French word. I cringed at the thought that her Mi'kmaq ancestry was also debased, ridiculed even, almost to the point of extinction. It is so very difficult to believe that many families of the Bay St. George area, on the west coast of Newfoundland, had to endure some of the above abuses to bring us to where we are today. Last, but certainly not least, I learned how, in her early 20's, my mother had to pack up her belongings, leaving her new house and home. Like all the other families around her, *Back of the Pond* liviers had to be expropriated from their properties in order to make room for the American Base in the early 1940's, during WWII. She, like the others, would never again see their beloved Paradise as they remembered it. Today, I envision my mother, not only as fragile and weak, but also as a feisty Acadian pioneer, a representation of our past. In spite of her many struggles, she was passionate in her role as mother, she had a strong religious faith, and she fought a brave fight to the very end. She has been, and still remains, my inspiration.

In Memory Of

In memory of my parents, Patrick Benoit and Agnita LeBlanc.

Married September 11, 1941

Patrick Benoit	Agnita LeBlanc
Born Oct 21, 1911	Born March 15, 1919
Died Feb 10, 2005	Died June 22, 1972

BACK OF THE POND

In memory of my maternal grandparents, Thomas LeBlanc and Julianna LeBlanc.

Married August 18, 1904

Thomas LeBlanc	Julianna LeBlanc
Born March 9, 1878	Born July 6, 1881
Died 1940	Died May 23, 1926

BACK OF THE POND

In memory of my paternal grandparents, James Benoit and Mary-Ellen Cormier.

Married May 20, 1907

James Benoit	Mary Ellen Cormier
Born May 8, 1883	Born Nov 22, 1888
Died May 2, 1980	Died Aug 16, 1976

Preface

What started out as a coping mechanism to fill some hours while my husband was away working has, years later, resulted in this book. I'm so glad, now, that I chose writing. It has proven to be very therapeutic.

Writing always makes me feel good. It is one of the few activities that interests me, and that I find uplifting; another is music. Not only has my passion for writing been fulfilled, but writing has provided an escape from my somber moods. For me, it has been a win-win situation.

Introduction: History of Stephenville

Stephenville is a small town on the west coast of Canada's tenth province, Newfoundland and Labrador. Today, in 2017, it has a population of about 7500 people. Even though it is primarily English-speaking, it was not so until the arrival of the American base in 1941.

The Stephenville area was first inhabited by Aboriginal people: the Dorset, the Beothuk and the Mi'kmaq. The Mi'kmaq arrived from Nova Scotia in the late 1700s, followed by many French Acadians. An Acadian by the name of François Benoit was living in the Bay St. George area by 1790; he married Anne L'Official. Others came from both Cape Breton (Margaree, Chéticamp) as well as Îles de la Madeline (the Magdalen Islands), settling in Sandy Point (Bay St. George) in the 1840s and 50s, bringing surnames like Aucoin (now O'Quinn), Arsenault, Benoit (now Bennett), Bergeron (now Burchell), Blanchard, Boudreau, Bourgeois, Broussard (many became Bruce), Cheverie, Chiasson, Cormier, Delaney, Deveau, Doucet(te), Haché (now Gallant), Muise, Gaudet, LeBlanc (now White), Lejeune (now Young), LeLièvre, Longuepee and Poirier to the area. They asked the Bishop if they could have a French priest come to look after their little community and he sent Father Alexis Bélanger to join them. Later, when the people moved over to Bay St. George because Sandy Point was being dangerously eroded away, their small mission church became part of the church in Bay St. George.

The new settlers, along with others who had lived nearby, set up their homes from Kippens to Indian Head. These "liviers," as they referred to themselves, instinctively called their new home "Acadian Village." Later, that name evolved among them into *Back of the Pond*, referring to those who lived in back of Stephenville Pond. This is the area where my parents, Patrick Benoit and Agnita LeBlanc, lived as a couple for a very short time. It is also the area where both sets of my grandparents grew up and raised their families.

Chapter 1: Recollection of 50s and 60s

The first 24 years of my life revolved around two primary streets: West Street, where I lived, and Main Street, which is perpendicular to it. At the intersection of Main and West, adjacent to where St. Stephen's High, Elementary and Primary schools were once situated, stood *A.V. Gallant's Confectionery* store. It offered an array of delectable milk shakes, banana splits, sundaes, along with a seeming endless variety of confections to please the eye and quench the appetite.

A.V.'s was one of the few hangouts for teenagers in those times. Another hangout, but for a much shorter time, was Stan Gallant's restaurant, the *Chicken Burger* on West Street; possibly in the same spot where Mary Brown's is situated today.

Now, I know from experience that there is nothing like getting a good Newfie argument going, so I've dared, with a lot of help from friends and relatives, to take a shot at remembering the store fronts on Main Street. Even though my aim is for the 1950s and 1960s, two decades is a long time.

Many changes can take place in that amount of time; they certainly did here in Stephenville. Consequently, your recollection of Main Street Stephenville businesses and telephone numbers may, no doubt, differ from mine.

Main Street, as in the case in most towns, was the hub of Stephenville. It still is. A walk through Main Street in the 1950s and early 60s might have led you past the following businesses and attractions.

BACK OF THE POND

A list of stores heading East on Main Street North. The pictures that follow represent only a small collection of Store Fronts; some of the old 3digit telephone numbers are included. Photos 15 and 18 are courtesy of Peggy Gale-Bennett. The remaining photos are courtesy of Bill Pike and the Bay St. George Genealogical Society.

40. Blanche Brook Bridge
39. Brookside Taxi (225)
38. Banikin's Clothing (217, 218)
37. Ches Burt's Store (715)
36. Paul Boulos' Dry Goods (223)
35. Colbourne's Convenience
34. Shoe Repair
33. Furniture Store
32. Mike Silver's Restaurant
31. Mike Silver's Store
30. Apartments (unknown)
29. Dome Theatre
28. Hann Brothers Furniture
27. Irving's Clothing
26. Irving's Style Shop
25. Isaac's Hardware
24. Shave's Bakery
23. Russell's Service Station (738)
22. Food Centre
21. Oscar Yates Jewelry
20. Meade's Hardware (745)
19. Major's Restaurant (727)
18. Arlim's Company
17. Frank's Electrical
16. Ben's Pharmacy (221)
15. Bank of Montreal
14. Corner Brook Garage

13. Ford's Plumbing
12. Byrne's Shoe Store
11. Blue Star Restaurant
10. Service Taxi Stand
9. Pond's Store
8. Ruth's Hair Salon (rooms upstairs)
7. Bayview Restaurant
6. Rothman's Clothing
5. One Hour Martinizing
4. Russell's Plumbing
3. Eddie's Service Station (721)
2. Handy Andy Auto
1. Gallant's Hotel (723)

BACK OF THE POND

Photo 7: Bayview Restaurant

Photo 15: Bank of Montreal

Photo 18: Arlim's Company

Photo 23: Russell's Service Station

Photo 26: Irving's Style Shop

Photo 28: Hann Brothers Furniture

BACK OF THE POND

A list of stores heading East on the South Side of Main Street. All photos courtesy of Bill Pike and the Bay St. George Genealogical Society.

70. Gatehouse (U.S.A.F. Base Entrance)
69. U.S.A.F. Property Communication Towers
68. Eddy's Taxi (721)
67. Model Shoe Store
66. McLellan'sFurniture
65. Clover Club
64. Candlelight Restaurant
63. Ben's Provision Store (221)
62. Leo Kaplow Clothing (726)
61. Brown Derby Tavern
60. Radio Lunch
59. Kearney's Clothing (Fun Palace downstairs)
58. Wells' Warehouse (746)
57. Little New Yorker Hotel
56. Page Theatre
55. Power Motors
54. Hudson's Bay Company
53. Shop Rite Warehouse
52. Shop Rite Groceteria
51. Royal Bank of Canada (740)
50. Rexall Pharmacy
49. NFLD Telephone
48. Domino's Pizza
47. Red Rose Club
46. Rory Duffy's Garage
45. Tiptop Grill (Pool Hall upstairs)
44. Lidstone/Luscombe Plumbing
43. French's Esso Station
42. White's Hotel
41. A.V. Gallant's Store (724)

BACK OF THE POND

Photo 47: Red Rose Club

Photo 50: Rexall Pharmacy

Photo 65: Clover Club

BACK OF THE POND

Main Street Stephenville 1952
Courtesy of Bill Pike and the Bay St. George Genealogical Society

Main Street Stephenville 1950s
Courtesy of Bill Pike and the Bay St. George Genealogical Society

Main Street Stephenville 1957
Courtesy of Bill Pike and the Bay St. George Genealogical Society

Main Street Stephenville 1958 Parade
Visit of Queen Elizabeth and Prince Philip
Courtesy of Bill Pike and the Bay St. George Genealogical Society

BACK OF THE POND

Main Street Stephenville January 1959
Courtesy of Bill Pike and the Bay St. George Genealogical Society

Main Street Stephenville January 1959
Courtesy of Bill Pike and the Bay St. George Genealogical Society

BACK OF THE POND

Main Street Stephenville 1962
Courtesy of Bill Pike and the Bay St. George Genealogical Society

Main Street and West Street
Courtesy of Bill Pike and the Bay St. George Genealogical Society

At the intersection of Main and West, adjacent to where St. Stephen's High, Elementary and Primary schools were once situated, stood *A.V. Gallant's Confectionery* store (on the left).

BACK OF THE POND

For some odd reason, these are the specific things that pop into my mind about Main and West Street.

I would have been about twelve or thirteen at the time. My parents went to the *Shop Rite* for weekly groceries. It was close to Christmas, I believe, and someone stole $45 worth of groceries from the back of what we called my father, Patrick's, "paddy wagon" (1950 Chev Panel Truck). This was a major setback for my parents. $45 was a considerable amount back then, and there wasn't a lot of money to make a second purchase. I guess we did without our bag of fluffs (corn puff cereal) that week.

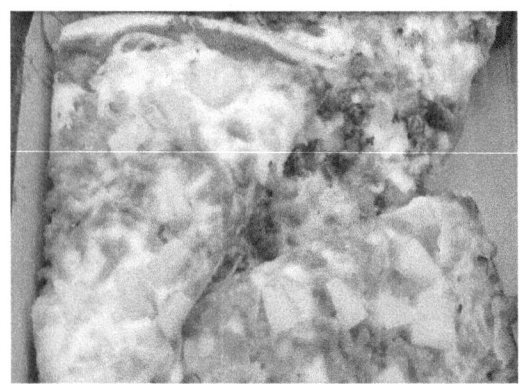

I met my husband in 1973. We met at a dance at *Cyril Gallant's Club* on West Street. I don't think I'd be wrong in saying that we had *Domino's Pizza* every night we dated, and for many years after. He should have been named the poster boy for the Pizza House. At that time, the Pizza House was one of a very few places where you could eat in or take out. It always drew large crowds, and still does so today.

Arlim's Company, still in business today, was renowned for the life-sized mechanical Santa Claus [1] displayed in its front glass window. This animated musical Santa was about six feet high and a delight for children to see. Because we were so used to the simple life, we waited in anticipation for the Christmas season. We looked forward to special treats such as candy,

---

[1] In the 50s and 60s we didn't have Santa visiting and posing for pictures as we do today; neither did the stores have toys on display all year around.

fruitcake, meat pies, cherry cake, Purity Syrup, cookies, etc., that we didn't get the rest of the year. I remember my brothers selling boxes of Hallmark Christmas Cards, in the months before Christmas, to make some spending money for the season or for gifts. This was done through mail order.

Everyone's Christmas tree was basically the same; the biggest your father or older brother could cut down, and be allowed, by your parents, to drag into the house and decorate.

There were no artificial trees at that time. We strung tinsel, garland and sometimes strings of popcorn. We hung bulbs; whatever we could afford to have. Chinese decorations were about all we could find in the stores. They were strung from one corner of the ceiling to the other, with maybe a bell in the middle.

On top of the tree, we placed an angel or a star to commemorate the birth of Christ on December 25. Christmas was one of the most celebrated days in the life of a child.

At midnight on Christmas Eve, the Catholic Church celebrated mass to mark the occasion, and after mass everyone would be eager to return home for meat pie (most always moose) and fruitcake. Before and after Mass, the night was full of activity; music, drink, food, and sometimes gift opening, depending on your age. More often, gifts were not opened until the morning after Santa came.

My home at 30 West Street was no hub, but it did have its share of mishaps, as all homes do. The following is an example of just one.

BACK OF THE POND

Carnation Milk definitely sustained us as children. What could be better than a bowl of fresh blueberries or strawberries, covered with sugar and pure Carnation Milk? I still like it today. As a child of about ten, I was home alone, for some reason, and decided to open that can of Carnation Milk to pour over my strawberries (fresh, hand-picked and wild), "like you would." I still can't visualize why I held onto the can with my left hand as I plunged the "little brown knife that cuts" into the can to punch hole number one; when I did, blood flew. I managed to dig the knife deep into the knuckle of my forefinger. I went screaming off across the lane to my Aunt Lena for help, who nursed my wound with blackstrap molasses, [2] taped my cut up tight and sent me on my way, good as new! It healed without a problem. I still have that beautiful scar today, as a reminder.

There are some things we're just not meant to forget, like the accident involving the milk can.

The same proves true with the sayings that my husband Bill recites from his younger years; they, too, are a testimony to the goodness of Carnation Milk, despite my misfortune with the can.

---

[2] Blackstrap Molasses contains Selenium, Vitamin B6, Magnesium, Calcium, Iron and other minerals and vitamins, which promote healthy skin and help combat stress. It helps to improve bone health, electrolyte balance, hair care, sexual health, functioning of the nervous system, and last, but not least, wound healing. Information from https://www.organicfacts.net/health-benefits/other/health-benefits-of-molasses.html

BACK OF THE POND

> *A cup of tea is not a cup of tea,*
>
> *No…….. sir!*
>
> *Not a cup of tea at all without Carnation.*

> *Carnation is the best of all.*
>
> *No tit to pull, manure to haul,*
>
> *Punch a hole, that's all.*

Upon further investigation of the above slogans, and not knowing whether or not it was appropriate to share the entry below without copyright, I came upon a claim about a lady from North Carolina. This lady, who had always lived on a family dairy farm, entered a five thousand dollar Carnation Milk Contest in 1911. The week after she sent it in, they drove up in front of her house in a black limousine and awarded her with a thousand dollar check because, although they weren't able to use the slogan, they loved her entry (which reads a little differently from my husband's rhyme).

> *Carnation Milk is best of all.*
>
> *No tits to pull, no shit to hall.*
>
> *No buckets to wash, no hay to pitch.*
>
> *Just poke a hole in the son-of-a-bitch.*

BACK OF THE POND

I cannot recall the Page Theatre; however, I do remember the Dome Theatre well. It seems to me that the Dome was a very old establishment when I walked through its doors in the 1960s. With its dim lighting, privacy, and mystique, the *Dome Movie Theatre* was the ideal setting for young lovers to make out.

I can still recall my first date for the movies. I believe I was thirteen years old. I dressed in pink slacks that my eldest sister Nina had sewn, a pink mohair sweater and my long thick hair French-twisted up. I walked from our family home on West Street to meet my date on Main Street.

We then walked to the Dome Theatre together, but because I was so shy and because he was so polite, I guess, I ended up in front of him in the pay line. Not knowing who should pay, rather than cause myself any more embarrassment, I automatically paid my own way and awkwardly refused to take his money afterwards. I think, though, he bought the popcorn. Remember, those were the days before women's liberation, [3] a time when guys paid the girl's way. But how was I to know? Poor Francis; forgive me if I stunted your ego that day. I realize now that such traumatic events (ha) can leave everlasting impressions.

Once past the Dome Theatre, one was getting intriguingly close to the bridge that separated American Army personnel from civilians. Across Blanche Brook Bridge was the site of Harmon Field, constructed in 1941.

Following that bridge was the entrance to the base through the Gatehouse.

---

[3] The Women's Liberation movement was an agreement of some women and feminist thinkers that emerged in developed countries during the late 1960s and persisted throughout the 1970s. Some women sought equal rights with men. I use the word liberation very loosely, as the 50s and 60s was a time before women paid their own way, before women opened their own doors, etc.

The Gatehouse

During, and in the aftermath of wartime, there was the new-found frolic of night life on base, and off base at clubs such as *Frenchie's*, the *Red Rose Club*, the *Clover Club* (or *Corral Club*), *Wheelers* and the *Dhoon Lodge*. The *Radar Installation Centre* at Pine Tree also had its share of music and dancing.

A walk down Main Street in my hometown in the 1950s and 60s might also give you occasion to meet an eccentric old man, or one who was always considered to be old because of his unkempt appearance. His long white beard, his slouched posture, his muttering to himself, his shabby clothes, all gave the outward appearance of being tired, tattered and aged.

Moses Murrin, also known as Mosey Burns, the man behind the façade, I remember, was an intriguing character; a witty, charming, yet frightening soul, possibly because there was so much about him that was unknown.

BACK OF THE POND

Draped in his ragged attire and pushing his wheelbarrow of garbage pickings, Mosey could be found most any day, rummaging through discarded wares, in search of the perfect addition to his wardrobe, or in search of any discarded item that could be salvaged for food, money or barter.

When I was a child, it was rumored that Mosey lived in a worn-down hut somewhere off the Hansen Highway. Some claimed he was rich, but kept his money stashed away among his wares and well hidden from view. I once heard he was shell-shocked during the war, after which he had begun to live like a crazy man, hoarding and stashing, but others, like my father, remember Mosey as a wise man, one with his wits about him and the ability to outsmart them all. A somewhat God-like creature, I thought, with baby blue eyes that twinkled brightly.

Mosey's well-being seemed to depend on social interaction and a need to entertain; he would knock on doors and ask to be fed. A bum or not, he loved fine food, hospitality, and an audience to tell intriguing stories and jokes to. He especially savored a kiss on the lips from the young girls *if* he could talk them into it. A peck, to my knowledge, is all he got as he jestered before young and old. And most of all, I remember that Mosey loved a good cup of loose tea, in a fancy cup and saucer, if you please, and nothing but your finest. Many a future was read from the tea leaves at the bottom of the cup.

As I said earlier, Mosey was a witty man and jokester. It was rumored that he was hanging around Harmon Base one day, when a ship came into the port. The ship's captain singled Mosey out and asked him, in an angry tone of voice, "Where are all the savages at?" (referring to the Mi'kmaq Indian population in the Bay St. George area at the time). Mosey immediately responded, "They're not all off the boat yet."

Another of my favorite Mosey jokes goes as follows.

BACK OF THE POND

There was a time when it was difficult to get alcohol, so many dabbled in the illegal practice of making and selling moonshine. When questioned by police, Mosey agreed that, for pay, he would release the name of the man who made the moonshine. After getting paid, he gladly revealed, "God made the moon shine bright."

Mosey was always something of a mystery, and remains so today in the eyes of many. He will forever be a legend of our time.[4] He died in 1980 at the age of 78.

In memory of Mosey, try the following Newfie joke on for size.

There once was a Newfoundland couple who had been married for ten years or so, but hadn't yet been successful in conceiving a child. Apart from a hearing problem, the wife seemed very healthy, and could think of no reason why she wasn't getting pregnant. After years of arguing and deliberation over who had the problem, the husband, "like he would," convinced his wife to see a doctor.

---

[4] The Ballad of Mosey Burns by Gerry Formanger located at
https://www.youtube.com/watch?v=Jq981lmI51s

BACK OF THE POND

A little reluctantly, "the wife," as most Newfoundland men refer to their wives, went to her doctor's appointment. The doctor did a thorough examination. Upon completion, and with compassion, he explained the sad news. He said, "You have an insufficient passage, and if you have any children, it would be a miracle." Mrs., of course, was very disturbed by the message she got from her gynecologist. Upon arriving home, she very reluctantly repeated to her husband what she had heard. The doctor told me, "I have a fish in my passage, and if I have any children, it will be a mackerel."

Just one more for the road. Can you guess the answer to this riddle?

I went in the woods and I got it

When I got it, I couldn't get it

So I left it

And I went home, and took it with me

The answer is located at the end of the Bibliography.

It wasn't illegal to make moonshine in the late 1950s or 1960s when Mosey was around, but in order to do so, you had to have a Federal license.

Moonshine still

Such licenses were very expensive, and a huge hassle to get. You could only make it in limited quantities for your own use. No doubt, the government did all they could to discourage the making and selling of moonshine, because it was potentially a much bigger money-maker than wine or beer. If left in the hands of the people versus government, the loss in taxes would have been immense.

I can recall my father having to travel to Corner Brook to purchase liquor. At that time (around the 1960s) he had to carry a liquor book, which had to be stamped when he made a purchase. Liquor must have been rationed at that time; clearly, there could not have been a liquor store in Stephenville yet.

BACK OF THE POND

I was still in high school when I began going to the *Fun Palace*. I remember watching others, a year or two older than me, dancing the jive for hours. I never did learn how to do that dance, even though my husband, who is four years older than me, can still dance it today. We danced to the jukebox, so, whoever put the quarter in first, got to choose the song.

A tall, handsome redhead from West Street would always play "Hey Jude," which is seven minutes and eleven seconds long, and ask me to waltz. I remember him being so much taller than me, and it was hard on my neck, but I was too embarrassed to tell him. I would never refuse a dance. He was a proper gentleman.

My friend Pauline and I went to the *Fun Palace* together. She was going to school with me at the time. I remember introducing her to my cousin Francis. They later married and currently reside in Kippens, with 4 children and 7 grandchildren.

At the *Fun Palace*, we "rocked" to the music of Chuck Berry, Fats Domino, Kitty Wells, Buddy Holly and others, such as Elvis Presley. Little did I realize, at that time, that some years earlier, Elvis had been in the Stephenville Airport, no more than a mile away.

In 1960, Sergeant Harry Eastus was on his three-year tour at the Ernest Harmon Air Force Base, in Stephenville, assigned to Flight Operations. The sergeant became aware of the fact that Elvis Presley was on a military aircraft, returning stateside, and would be stopping at the base for refueling at 0100 hours.

The Sergeant called his daughter, Harriet, who was president of the Elvis Presley Fan Club. He alerted her to the pending arrival, encouraging her to gather up her friends to meet Elvis. Harriet panicked (like you would) and left for the airport alone.

Even though the passenger terminal was practically full of onlookers, Harriet managed to get Elvis' undivided attention, plus a kiss on the cheek, and one on the lips. She was the envy of bobby sockers everywhere. It's quite ironic that, after leaving Elvis' homeland, the U.S.A., she got such a rare chance to meet her idol, "The King of Rock and Roll," in the small military town of Stephenville.

The King and I - Harriet McCullers (nee Eastus) clutches her camera and autograph book as she poses with Elvis Presley, the King of Rock and Roll, during his stopover at Ernest Harmon Air Force Base in Stephenville, NL on March 2, 1960.

BACK OF THE POND

When I was in my teens, and interested in hanging out with my friends, we sometimes went to the *Blue Star Restaurant* on Main Street. We would sit in the booths, and order fries, hamburger and a Coke (if we had enough money). Those three items were the big sellers. That may have cost a total of 25 cents, but that amount was very much out of my reach, most of the time.

I was about 11 years old, walking through Main Street, across from the *Tip Top Grill*, when an old man (about 22 years old) by the name of Willy Pluck Pluck, whom some said was a little bit silly, called out from across the street, asking if he could buy me a small coke and grilled cheese sandwich. I immediately blurted "no thanks," and just walked away as quickly as I could, hoping desperately not to draw more undue attention to myself. I was petrified.

I can sadly recall the "wake" of two young boys, each 16 years of age. I walked with some friends through Main Street until we turned left where the Blue Bird Taxi Stand is today. The street is now named Provincial Street. At the end of that street, or somewhere in that vicinity, there were two houses across from each other. I seem to recall, although my memory is a little sketchy, wakes taking place at the same time at those two houses.

I didn't know either of those boys, although they were just a year older than me. I do recall, however, that they had died in a car that went over the bank in Felix Cove on the Port au Port Peninsula, landing on the ocean rocks below. Their names were Floyd White and Cyril White. My friends and I prayed for the boys and comforted each other. Teenagers always banded together and supported each other in times of crisis.

I can remember another incident when I was walking through Main Street on my way home. We walked everywhere. It was unheard-of for one of my brothers or sisters to ask for a ride. I enjoyed walking. Actually, it gave me something to do. On this day, though, I would have been better off at home.

BACK OF THE POND

There was a large group of people gathering along the side of Main Street, very close to where The Bar is now; back then it was called the *Red Rose Club*. Like the onlookers, I glanced as I passed by, wondering what the commotion was about. Lying there by the street was a young boy who had, it appeared, been hit by a car. Someone had him covered with a blanket or some clothes so I could not see, not even his face. I said prayers for him as I walked toward home. Later, I learned that his last name was Barry, and that he had lived nearby. I also heard he died that same day.

Our house was very close to Bernard and Lillian Gaudon's. They had a daughter, Joyce-Ann, their oldest. Very book-smart, Joyce-Ann was on the honor roll throughout school at St. Stephen's. She won a scholarship to continue her education at a prestigious university. It was nearing the end of the school year. My brother, Vernon, had been her escort to the prom. In her final weeks at school, Joyce-Ann took sick, developed pneumonia and died. She was probably only sixteen years old at the time.

I have just one more memory of Joyce-Ann to share with you. Walking home from school, one day, she came up close behind us. We were a few years younger than her and she uttered, to our dismay, a word none of us could even recognize nor pronounce. The word we clearly heard was "supercalifragilisticexpialidocious."

Joyce-Ann was waked at home on Colonial Avenue. I remember visiting with a large number of boys and girls of all ages, coming and going. It was such a sad occasion; one I cannot easily forget.

When we were children, wakes in Stephenville were held in the homes. Three chairs were lined up on either side and a white sheet spread covering the chairs. The open casket was set down on the chair seats for support. The person was waked in his home for two full days and nights. Someone would keep a vigil at all times.

BACK OF THE POND

My father said that in his younger days, the whole community would come to the wakes. At these wakes, food was always served. Everyone would bake and cook to bring some food offerings; large or small. There was no need for the immediate family of the deceased to cook. The community would take over that role. Also, the coffin and the cross would usually be made by a close family member; uncle, brother, close friend, etc. As was also customary, the grave would be dug by relatives or close friends, and graves filled in after the burial service by the same. As he grew older, Dad told us, things began to change; there were funeral homes, crematoriums, etc.

Chapter 2: Mona

Like most people, I guess, I have foggy memories of my childhood years. The earliest I remember seems to have been around five or six years of age. One clear childhood memory brings me back to a game of hide-and-go-seek in the tall grass in our backyard at 30 West Street. I remember this cute, blonde-haired boy, Butch, and how my cousin, Mona, stole his heart away from all her cousins, friends and sisters. No matter where she hid, he found her before any of us.

Specific memories of Mona seem easier to recall than others. She died at the age of nine, leaving me to feel the trauma of death at an early age. She was such a big part of my life. Being the same age, and living next door to each other, we were like sisters. We were together almost every day.

When Mona hurt her back in a fall, I laughed hysterically, because I thought she was faking. I recall now the daring game we had played. Boys and girls alike, we took our turns climbing up one tree, and crossing over half way to another tree. We did this by hand, along a horizontal pole from which we swung and jumped.

The structure we jumped from resembled that of a swing set, but without the swings in place. For a young child, a climb and jump was a bold gesture, one no doubt egged on by peer pressure. On that day in particular, though, it proved dangerous, and we would play it for the last time.

After falling from the pole, Mona was carried into her house by her father. She was then taken to hospital, and returned home some hours later with bandaged ribs. That was a scary sight for a young child like me to witness. I went home full of guilt and shame for having laughed earlier.

BACK OF THE POND

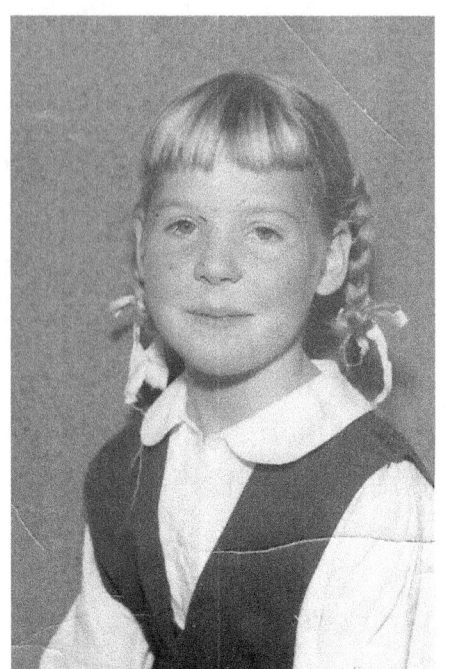

Mercedes Benoit-Penney age 7

I started Grade 1, at St. Stephen's Primary School on West Street, when I was around six years old. We always walked to school. We went home for dinner at 12 o'clock, returning at 1 o'clock for afternoon classes.

I hated school. It was very formal, very strict and unforgiving. As a child, I felt alone and always afraid.

Our teachers, the Presentation Sisters, or nuns as we called them, wore thick straps hanging down from their waists, and they didn't fail to use those straps if someone disobeyed their rules, or rubbed them the wrong way.

I was so traumatized from my first year in school that the fear remained with me, and was continually reinforced, until I graduated Grade 11. I had the occasional lay teacher, but the Presentation Nuns remained in the school system throughout elementary and high school.

Mona Benoit age 7

When we started school, with the nuns as our teachers, I was completely devastated that Mona was not among my classmates. There were two Grade 1 rooms, separated by folding doors; she was in one room, I was in the other.

BACK OF THE POND

L – R: Convent, St. Stephen's High School, St. Stephen's Elementary,

St. Stephen's Primary attached to Elementary School facing West Street (circa 1962)

Picture courtesy of Bill Pike and Bay St. George Genealogical Society

From day one, I hated school. I hated the boy behind me for pulling my pigtails. I hated the fear of the unknown that seemed to grip each one of us. I despised the strict rules that were a part of the Catholic system and the lonely feelings that I felt in that silent classroom of forty or more children. In fact, I hated school so much, I would hide out in places between home and St. Stephen's Primary.

I don't remember how I passed the hours, or even if I managed to pull it off, but it was an obsession with me to avoid school. I'd leave my books behind a telephone pole along West Street to avoid suspicion when I returned home for dinner. [5] Can you imagine? After dinner, I'd return to the telephone pole until afternoon classes were over, or until someone found me out, which probably wasn't difficult to do.

---

[5] In parts of the United States, supper and dinner are used interchangeably to refer to the evening meal, but here in Newfoundland, dinner has always been the mid-day meal for us (akin to lunch), and supper the evening meal. In Newfoundland we traditionally have three meals, breakfast, dinner and supper.

BACK OF THE POND

Once, I hid my school uniform in the bottom of an old rum barrel of skates in our store house (aka the shed). In the company of moose quarters hanging from the rafters, and barrels of salt capelin for the taking, the skate barrel, I guessed, was the last place someone would look.

Mine was the ultimate plan, or so I thought. St. Stephen's Primary School had strict rules, one being that you never went to school unless you wore the traditional school uniform: the navy tunic, with white blouse underneath. I don't remember the outcome of that bold gesture. As I said earlier, my memories are foggy, but I believe that was the day my mother decided to visit the nuns at the convent in my defense, or maybe it was the day she offered me a twenty-five cent piece if I went back to school.

BACK OF THE POND

I always felt that Mom was sympathetic to my feelings, but like most other parents at that time, she rarely, if ever, questioned decisions made by the authority of the day; the clergy and/or the Catholic system. Sympathetic or not, I felt completely alone in my new school setting. I didn't fit in. I was extremely shy. I got sick often and as I got older, I justified feeling like a lost soul by believing the motto instilled in us by all (the nuns, the priests and Mom) that "suffering, hard work, and pain brought one closer to heaven."

It would never have occurred to me to tell my parents or anyone else how I felt. I wasn't sure how I felt. I only knew that when I went to school, on this particular day, my cousin Mona wasn't with me. Upset, my first inclination was to kick a nun in the shins, a gesture I'm proud of today. Then, I was running full pelt toward home, and trying to free myself from a big strapping boy, Lloyd, who was sent by the nuns to carry me back. I would be dragged back just a short distance from the school, screaming and hollering, to face the consequences.

I don't recall the consequences; another blank in my memory. I sound like a tough one, I know, but let me assure you, I wasn't. I mellowed somewhat after that, but not before Mom took me to talk to the school principal or Mother Superior, as the highest-ranking nun of the convent was called. We stood on the convent steps. My mother explained how I needed to be in class with someone I knew. I admired Mona, had grown up with her, and felt so secure when she was around. The nun promised that a change would be made, and that we would be placed in the same classroom. I believed what I heard. I went home full of hope, with a reason to go to school every day, and kept believinguntil I grew accustomed to the school day without her. The principal never did keep her promise.

On October 13, 1960, Mona, at the age of nine, was run over by a car on West Street.

BACK OF THE POND

It was a horrible, rainy night. Mona, her older sister Doreen, and a close friend, Betty-Jean, were on their way to Benediction, a weekly prayer service that took place at 7:30 pm each Wednesday evening at St. Stephen's Catholic Church. Because it was raining, I hadn't been allowed to go to church with them that night. We had always walked together. As a member of the choir, and dearly loving to sing, above all else, I was drawn to the church for most services.

When I heard the sad news, I hid away in my bedroom to cry. I wouldn't have felt comfortable showing such emotion in front of my family. When my eldest sister Nina offered me chocolates to cheer me up a little, I refused to accept them. Even though chocolates were a rare treat, and surely would have given me great pleasure, I was afraid that accepting them would immediately send out the wrong message, trivializing the importance of Mona's death. I really couldn't believe that God would let someone die in their attempts to go to church and worship him.

Back then, I found Mona's death difficult to understand and accept. Looking back at it today, it seems such a normal consequence in the whole scheme of things. I tell myself that, after all, every one of us dies, sooner or later; yet, her death seemed to have taken such a big chunk of my good childhood memories away. Although, on the one hand, it seemed like a minor consequence to the world, it was major in my little world. You know, as much as I can recall about Mona, I can't remember her wake or her funeral mass. I can only recall walking away from the graveyard on West Street after the burial.

In retrospect, I was, on October 13, 1960, seeing from a nine-year-old point of view. I didn't understand how anything could remain normal after my cousin's death. Her passing, from my childhood perspective, appeared to be made light of. My hope from that time on was that a much higher power must exist, one that never makes light of anything that transpires here on earth.

Mona Benoit, First Holy Communion

Chapter 3: Margie

Stop laughing, Margie!

Margie was a very dear friend of mine through high school. I was afraid she would discover how insecure I felt because I thought everyone could see right through me. I thought everyone could see all of my flaws. As a result, I kept my guard up real high, for fear of getting burned. I have yet to understand why I was like that, especially with her. I see now that I was afraid to give my undivided trust. I wasn't completely honest with Margie. I owe her an apology. I lied to her.

Margie and I spent endless hours studying, playing, singing and listening to music, showing our devotion to God, smoking, and, last but not least, laughing. I'd say that the number of hours devoted to laughing far outweighed all other activities. Having had the opportunity to reflect on those years, I definitely have to conclude that laughter was my savior.

Getting back to apologizing for not being honest to Margie, our parents, thank goodness, gave us the freedom to study together on weeknights. We studied for hours, laughing all the while, associating schoolwork with everyday life as much as we could; anything to help us remember what we had read. Never before were our marks so high. We achieved wonders in school. Finally, there was a payoff for the endless hours of dedication to the books.

I had always overindulged in my schoolwork, never being involved in sports or other extracurricular activities. Unlike my younger brother Tommy, I had to study very hard just to get by. Study as I might, certain things like Math just wouldn't sink in on their own. So, when Margie asked me if I used to study on the side after she went home at night, of course I didn't give my secret away. I often spent another two hours cramming after she left. I never, ever lacked the quality of stick-tuitiveness. I just rarely got a reward for my efforts.

BACK OF THE POND

We were just as dedicated in our commitment to our religion. There was an unwritten rule among the community, that young people should do their share of duty to the church; but as straight-faced as one might be, going into that building, there was something about a quiet, sacred place that made me and my friend laugh.

The laughter would come at the most inopportune time: during a Benediction service, the moment the priest was giving his sermon, the moment the bladder wouldn't safely hold its contents, or while reading private requests that had been left in the novena box by others. Suffice it to say that there were numerous occasions when I wet my clothes from laughing too hard.

There was one evening, in particular, that the priest singled me out in the middle of a service, scolding me in front of the whole congregation; that evening, I didn't wet my clothes, but I'm sure I turned a shade of grey, shortly after I turned a brighter shade of crimson. That would not happen again. Not the blushing, of course, but the laughing during Benediction.

As for the wetting, I had little or no control over that. I still don't, much. There was no washroom in that old church. The trip home was more than a kilometer and access to a washroom was hard to come by. At least once, I peed on the floor of the old church porch because it was just too cold to do so outside. Sorry to offend, but keep in mind that I was just a child.

Margie, I've come a long way since those diary additions when I was twelve or thirteen years old. I've extended my vocabulary somewhat. I no longer use phrases like, "I had lots of fun," "today I rode my bike," or "today I went to the store" to express a full day's events. But those diary additions made you laugh so much. I'm glad some good came of them.

BACK OF THE POND

These were the children in my neighbourhood. It looks like this was a Schumph party. I am in the third row. Can you recognize anyone? I've been searching for Margie's picture.

I can't help but also mention the day we were smoking in my bedroom and made a great discovery. Although smoking was the fad in those years, it was still off-limits to us teenagers. I remember learning to smoke in my Uncle Luke's outhouse with my cousin Lillian. Outhouses were outdoor toilets, such as are used at the parks today.

There were quite a few outhouses left at that time, as the transition was being made from outside to inside. We used to pick discarded cigarette butts off the ground. We may have inadvertently borrowed a cigarette or two from our father's packs. Cigarettes were easy to come by at that time; just about everyone smoked and was unaware of their danger.

For weeks, maybe months, we raised my bedroom window and blew the smoke outside, or so we thought. One day, Margie, who always appeared super smart to me, pointed out that the cigarette smoke was coming back into the room through the top of the window.

BACK OF THE POND

The laughter started, as we realized that a storm window, as it was called, was completely blocking off any cold from entering the room, or anything else from leaving the room, for that matter. Houses at that time were not well-insulated, so every means to keep out the cold was utilized. In fact, our storm windows stayed up all year round. I guess for the short summers we had, it didn't make much sense to remove them, only to put them back in a few months.

Needless to say, Margie and I went through a range of emotions in a very short time, especially me. First, the laughter, that our cigarette smoke was now finding its way through every conceivable crack or cranny around the inside window, especially through the large space at the bottom, where we had it raised. Second, there was the dread that I would surely get caught by my mom at any minute. I had visions of that smoke hovering below and above my door and outside in the hallway. I envisioned the smell of smoke making its way to Mom's nose. I could imagine the light bulb that would go on in her head as she discovered that her unblemished daughter had committed a venial, if not mortal, sin. From dread, my thoughts turned to fear, as I didn't even want to imagine the punishment for such a crime. Next, the feelings of guilt set in. Why was I so stupid as to get caught? I certainly would never do that again. That feeling of guilt hurt way too much.

What was I to do now? Even my friend couldn't help me with this one. There would be confession: "Oh God ... please let this horrible feeling leave me ... I promise ... I'll never, ever, ever ... be so stupid again ... as to get caught!"

Chapter 4: Those Trying School Days

Those trying school days were unfortunately more trying for some than for others. My brother Tommy, a year younger than me, can vouch for what I say. Tommy always had a cute baby face which made him easy to love and easy to forgive. Late homework, stanzas un-memorized, idleness in the classroom; one look at that cute face and all was forgiven. But for me, things were different. While Tommy played the usual boyhood games outdoors, I spent all my evenings memorizing, reading and working out Math problems, still believing that "practice makes perfect." Not in all cases, I soon learned. The more I studied, the less I seemed to understand. I always missed the big picture. I know now that I read too deep into what I studied. If I understood a stanza of poetry, after the first reading, I couldn't believe it could be so easy, so I would read much more into it, until I lost the main idea all together.

For most of my school years, I was afraid to speak up. In fact, I felt really dumb. I often thought I knew the answer to a question, but I would never say it for fear of being wrong. The answer I had in mind seemed too simple. "If that was right," I reasoned, "someone else would have said it by now." Mind you, once the correct answer was given, I felt like kicking myself for not speaking up earlier. Over and over, I repeated the same mistake, for fear I would look or sound stupid before my classmates or my teacher. Now, of course, I realize that most of the children in my class didn't know any better than I did. They too were afraid to be wrong. They, too, were sometimes shy or uneasy about the consequences of being wrong. Like me, they also had a fear of being laughed at. My fear was reinforced when, during my turn at reading aloud in school, I read "the old gentleman had a long black beard" mispronouncing beard to sound like bird.

BACK OF THE POND

On one occasion in Grade 10, Tommy and I went to school as usual. I had my French homework completed but Tommy didn't. This year, even though we weren't the same age, we were in the same grade together, because I had failed the year before. Once again, I had spent hours making sure my school homework was prepared for the next day. Like all the days before, Tommy had played outdoors, spent very little time on his schoolwork, no time on French homework, and then went off to school on his wit and charm. French class resumed. Tommy was two rows to my right, seated towards the back of the class. Our French teacher, a nun, walked up and down each row of seats, starting on my side of the room, making her way to me first, and then to Tommy a little later. On this occasion, I got brushed over quickly because my work was not only correct, but neatly prepared. I sat proudly, albeit somewhat nervously, in my seat.

Some nuns had the ability to send shivers down your spine; this one, in particular, topped the list. She was a heavy-set woman, tall, with big bone structure and weighed well over 200 pounds. It was very intimidating to see her heavy stature sway towards me. Her large leather strap [6] hung down a foot or more from her waist and dangled from her side. When she reached Tommy's desk, she was a little out of earshot; yet I could faintly hear her ask him why he hadn't completed his French homework. He responded in his usual charming way that he didn't know how to do the work. "Why didn't you ask your sister for help?" asked the nun. "Well," Tommy hesitated a little, "she was too busy studying and I didn't want to bother her."

---

[6] Standard straps were made of stitched leather, over a foot long, a couple of inches or so wide, and half an inch thick. Retrieved from
http://bloodandtreasure.typepad.com/blood_treasure/2009/05/strapping-young-men.html

The nun continued her homework check on the rest of the class. When she had finished with the last student, she asked to see me outside the classroom door. There, she strapped my hands numerous times with her thick strap. As she put it, I should have known Tommy could use my help. I should have offered it to him without his asking. In her eyes it was my fault that he hadn't completed his homework. He was free to go unpunished.

NATURE DENIED NUN TOO SOON

Situations that denied all sense of reasoning, like the above, were commonplace in our school. Most of the Presentation Sisters that I encountered were far from kind and sympathetic. Those that were, probably received little credit. Rather, most of the nuns ruled with a heavy fist and a harsh demeanor. They appeared to hate their job as teachers and/or administrators, as well as the children under their care.

The main focus of the religious order was supposed to be on spiritual development. To complete the requirements of the order, the sisters were expected to fulfill the final religious vows of poverty, chastity and obedience; thus, these young women, probably in their late teens or early twenties, had to suppress the urge to acquire worldly goods that other young women would want; things that lift our spirits, such as nice clothes, hairdos, etc. They had to suppress basic human urges or tendencies towards boys their age, the need for relationships that help build self-esteem, the need to love and be loved. And finally, they always had to adhere to the rules and regulations laid down by the church. These vows served to control the actions and behaviors of the nuns in such a dramatic way that it would be stifling for some, and almost inevitably, must have been overwhelmingly stressful. It is not surprising, then, that many of them behaved the way they did.

BACK OF THE POND

Psychotherapist and former Benedictine priest A.W. Richard Sipe noted in an essay from 2010 that there is "great loneliness, depression and emotional stress that can come from struggling with prolonged celibacy." [7] Maybe there is some truth in these words because Pope Francis suggested in a 2012 interview that the Vatican stance on celibacy might change in the near future.

Adding to their discomfort, the Presentation Sisters must have felt over-dressed, to say the least. They were weighted down with layers of clothing and religious paraphernalia that they wore every time they were in public. They dressed in a black tunic that draped to the floor; the tunic was covered by a scapula, an apron that hung down in back and front, and tied under the belt. They also wore a tight-fitting white cap called a coif which was itself covered by a black veil. On the black woven belt around their waist hung a rosary of wooden beads, and a long leather strap, often made of horsehide. A cross of silver was traditionally hung around their neck on a long black cord, and a simple silver ring worn on the left hand symbolized that their final religious vows had been taken. Unadorned black shoes complimented the habit or wardrobe of the day. And let's not forget the undergarments that must have been warm and cumbersome, especially in summertime. As well, there were the plastic-coated headbands or forehead bands and/or extra sleeves of different lengths that could be attached for special occasions. Some clothing varied among different religious orders, and positions taken within those orders.

The life they led must also have been a lonely one. I would rarely see the nuns walk around the school grounds. Never did I see one of them leave the grounds to walk on West Street. Following a very strict regimen, they were obviously encouraged to keep a safe distance from members of the public.

Using Webster's English Dictionary, as well as Wikipedia and other online dictionaries, I have put together a definition of the word "laity" that I can now make more sense of. In the past, I'll admit, I never did know that nuns were laypersons, that they are defined by some as ordinary people.

---

[7] https://www.ncronline.org/blogs/examining-crisis/reality-celibate-life-reflections-henri-nouwen

In fact, I never thought of nuns and priests as being distinct from one another; rather, I looked at them as an entity. However, research has shown that I was wrong. I now know that the clergy only constitutes the body of all people who have been ordained for religious duties (priests, bishops, deacons and ministers).

The laity, on the other hand, are both ordinary people (as opposed to the clergy) as well as non-ordained people like nuns, who take vows of chastity, obedience and poverty.

According to the clergy, the laity, in the eyes of the Lord, were a lesser form of life, and different from the clergy, because they were ordinary members of the public.

In my opinion, many of the nuns took their vocations far too seriously. My French teacher, the one I spoke of earlier, had told our class that because she was doing God's work in the school, she was indeed taking God's place; therefore, she was God and demanded to be treated like God himself. We had to kiss her hand and bow to her, whenever she expected us to.

DOUBLE JEOPARDY

Once, in elementary school, I had one of my sisters for a teacher. For some reason, that day is the only day of that particular school year that I seem to remember; it sticks out prominently in my mind. I was eleven or twelve years old. It was an honor to be chosen to perform even the most menial of tasks for the teacher, especially if you got the rare chance to leave the classroom. This day, for whatever reason, it was my turn to walk down to the far end of the hallway and empty the waste paper basket into a much larger garbage bin. I was especially shy and impressionable around my big sister, Linda, and I was eager to do a good job to make her proud of me. I had only recently learned that she *was* my sister; my grandparents had raised her, for reasons I was too young to understand. I only remember feeling excited and proud at the news. My new sister became somewhat of a novelty to me and my brother Tommy, when we finally found out. This school year was the perfect chance for us to bond a little. I was thrilled, uplifted and exhilarated by the idea of having my very own sister for a teacher. It had

BACK OF THE POND

happened before, in Grade 2, but that had been years ago. My sister, Nina, the eldest of the family, had been my teacher for half time in Grade 2. That had been exciting as well. I was so shy, even with her, that I wouldn't accept a full bottle of 7-Up (that I dearly loved) to revive me from a fainting spell that I had one day in school. I got sick often, that year in Grade 2.

I was a big girl now. With pride, I entered the hallway. With wastebasket in hand, I made my way along the corridor toward the bin at the far end. As I reached the middle of the hallway, I came face and eyes into the principal of our school, as well as a number of parents who were, I later learned, visiting the school for Education Week. Immediately upon seeing me, the principal brought me to a halt. She demanded, in an accusing and scolding manner, that I go back the way I came, and not parade around with garbage in front of the parents. Confused, I stood for a second with my mouth hanging open, wondering what I had done wrong. Then, out of fear, it occurred to me that I might have to disobey my teacher, my sister. On returning down the corridor, I had a brainstorm of an idea. I had figured out, all by myself, how to kill two birds with one stone. I could obey my teacher, yet not be seen in front of the parents with the garbage, which the principal *had* pointed out as being the main problem. Right?

At the far end of the hallway, toward which I was now heading, was a stairway to the second floor. I could climb the stairs, walk the hallway above and still empty the waste basket without being seen. What a brilliant idea! On my merry way I went, up the stairs, along the hall, and lo and behold, who did I run into again? The same group of people as before, principal and all. They, too, had climbed the stairs. It had never occurred to me that they might be touring the whole school. I was scolded harshly in front of all parties for defying the authority of a *principal*, marched back to my classroom, stood in front of my classmates and strapped numerous times for being so disobedient. That harness leather strap on the hands wasn't nearly as painful as the sting of humiliation and shame I felt that day. I felt as if my whole world came tumbling down around me. Quite a bonding my sister and I made that day, for sure. And for what? I still don't fully understand what I did that was so wrong.

BACK OF THE POND

DRAMA CLASS: "SHOTS FIRED!"

My cousin, Theresa, loved to put on a show; anything to make us laugh. Thank God for her antics. I'm not sure I would have made it through those dreadful school days without her. Theresa was dating a boy, Wayne, who went to the amalgamated school, so that was another "no-no" already. "Roman Catholics *fraternizing* with *non*-Catholics; out of the question."

Anyway, this story is not about religion. Theresa was in row one of our classroom, overlooking the beach. I believe she was in the second seat from the front. I was in the third row, maybe halfway down, with a good view of her. Wayne, we assumed, mooched from school to go target shooting on the beach. The class lesson had begun; the nun was in prime gear with everyone's undivided attention. Just as she finished her sentence, a shot rang out. Everyone went on high alert, and, without a second of warning, Theresa fell 'dead' over her seat. We all stared in amazement and shock. About fifteen seconds had gone by when Theresa picked herself up, readjusted her position and looked up at the nun as though nothing had taken place. A few minutes later, the scene was repeated. Another shot, another fall. This continued until Theresa grew tired, or Wayne ran out of ammunition. To a class of students never allowed to do anything out of line, this was hilarious. To some of us, it still is. To those of you who don't find the humor in this, as the saying goes, "you just had to be there."

WHEREFORE ART THOU, MYRON?

As much as a strapping on the hands hurt, it wasn't nearly as hurtful as another incident in high school. I remember that day well. I was seated in the last row in the back of the class. Directly across from me was Myron. We were talking, giggling; who knows, maybe even flirting. One thing I do know, it would take little more than the drop of a hat to embarrass me, or shame me in front of him, or the rest of my classmates. I was at a very vulnerable age, was very shy, and did nothing, absolutely nothing, to draw attention to myself. It was between classes. To save time and confusion, the teachers, rather than the students, exchanged rooms.

BACK OF THE POND

It was only natural that we sneak a couple of minutes to talk, laugh and be idle, after we had exchanged books and prepared for the next subject. On this day, however, for whatever reason, it was again my turn to be singled out.

The nun walked into the room and up to the front of the class, where she dropped her books on the desk. Without hesitation, and without warning, she made her way to the row where I sat, walked quickly to my seat and slapped me across the face. Stunned by the blow, I had difficulty composing myself for a few seconds. I didn't know, in fact, what had happened, why I was slapped or what to do next. She then proceeded to mumble on about my brazen attitude, my rudeness in class, my insolence. She demanded that I look at her when she spoke, yet she slapped me the second time because of the way I looked at her. I was really in trouble now. I remember thinking, "How do you want me to look at you? You just slapped my face for no reason." And believe me, I did my very best to please her, to do as she said. I was scared and humiliated, embarrassed enough to want to die right there, but as hard as I tried that day, it wasn't enough. She slapped my face over and over, each time repeating, "now look at me like that again, and you'll get another slap." Finally, that nun gave up. She left me red-faced, heartbroken and in tears to face the rest of the day, amid the stares and pity of my classmates.

Myron, like me, was just a young teenager, but I wondered, at the time, why he didn't stand up for me. I know now that it was unfair of me to expect him to do so. I later learned that the boys could defend themselves well, in front of the nuns, but they were just as vulnerable in the hands of some male members of the staff or the male bureaucracy that existed outside the school; namely, the clergy. Boys, from an early age, no doubt, learned to keep out of trouble as much as possible, for fear of being disciplined by the priest or his counterparts. Bureaucracy was difficult to contend with at that time.

Chapter 5: And Why French, Oh Lord!

And why French, oh Lord! Why do so many bad memories revolve around French classes? My father, Patrick Benoit, born in 1911, was French-speaking; he clearly remembers being strapped for speaking his native language in school. Unable to speak English at first, he and numerous others suffered a great deal at the hands of the lay teachers or clergy, for the short school life that many of them had. My father left school at the age of twelve to cut logs at Camp 45, one of the wood camps behind Deer Lake. Leaving school in 1923, he remembered the changeover from French to English.

My uncle Andrew, my father's brother, told me that when they were children, all their French books were removed from their school overnight, without notice, and replaced with English books. The next morning, they were not allowed to speak any more French, only English. If they spoke French, they were punished. He noted that many bruises were inflicted, and the occasional finger broken, when the dreaded stick was used to keep the tongue in line.

Dad recalled one story of how he was hit hard on the head by Monsignor Adams. As the story went, he was just a boy, holding hands with his friends at school, playing a child's game. Dad knew very little English, but was not allowed to speak any French. He must have accidentally let a French word slip out. Monsignor Adams, upon hearing him do so, almost knocked my father over with a hard smack to the back of the head.

Remember, French was their mother tongue. School was very difficult for them with these new expectations. I don't know the reason for the language change; I can only speculate. The hiring of teachers at that time was done by the clergy, so it wasn't unusual for the parish priest to make occasional visits to the little one-room school, bearing his harness-leather strap for those who were difficult to "discipline."

BACK OF THE POND

Back of the Pond School – 1940 or 1941

Front Row L – R: Martha March (7); Zita March (6); Genevieve White (6); Doreen White (7); Ramona O'Neill (7); Olive O'Neill.

2nd Row: Include Miss Wade and the child in front of her, not the girl in black sweater/white buttons.

L – R: Vivian White; Antoinette White (11); Edna White (15); Gloria White (12); Sis Russell; Joan March (12); Zita White and Teacher (Miss Wade).

Back Row L – R: Muriel White; Theresa White; Lillian White; Regina White; Ann O'Neill (12); Blanche Russell; Pauline White (14) and Ann Russell.

The one-room "Stephenville Pond School" was located approximately one mile from my grandfather Benoit's house. It was four miles to the nearest school run by the nuns, so children out of walking distance had the privilege of attending the Pond School instead.

As impractical as it was, discipline in harsh form was doled out by doctrinaires like the parish priest and/or many teachers who worked under the priest's jurisdiction.

BACK OF THE POND

NOT STUN ENOUGH, EH?

By the time I went to school, that same structure of harsh discipline was still in effect; strappings would be doled out daily by our teachers, our instructors, our educators. What knowledge did they impart on our young minds? One of my teachers, a layperson, had her own unique, warped, method of disciplining our minds and bodies to follow her rules. Her expectations were of perfection. Being a student of average ability, my marks in French rarely earned me any stars on the chart for excellence. On one such test, I got the usual 57 per cent or so, as did the majority of the class. Then there were those who didn't quite reach the 50 per cent mark, and another small minority who got close to reaching perfection. As usual, our names were called aloud. The marks were announced for all to hear; each student dropped back into his seat to contemplate the mark assigned, and the comments given, on their paper by the teacher.

Then came the dreaded sound of silence from the class, as our French teacher gave her usual lecture. Next would come the punishment, the strapping on the hands and forearms. Since all of these methods had failed to produce 100 per cent from her students, our "beloved teacher" elected to try a new approach this day. One after the other, she singled out all students whose marks fell in the 80 and "above" category. This day, contrary to what everyone expected, she strapped each of those students, giving the greater number of straps to the ones with the highest marks, and lessening the number of straps as she went down the line. Her reasoning was, that if you were smart enough to get between 80 and 99, then you were smart enough to get 100. The lesser your mark, obviously the lesser your ability, she reasoned, and thus, for that day at least, undeserving of punishment. For a change, I had lucked out.

RAMPSING AND ROLLING LIKE TRUE NEWFOUNDLANDERS

Surely there were some happy times, you ask? Well, of course! I certainly don't mean to dwell on the negative aspects of my school days. I can recall, rather vividly, at least two such occasions worth mentioning. One took place in a Grade 9 classroom that consisted solely of girls.

BACK OF THE POND

In our class was one student who was unknown to everyone; she had just come to our area recently and was somewhat of a misfit. Rumors quickly circulated that she had been abused by her parents, locked out in the cold, removed from her parent's home. The class had no problem befriending her. Treated with respect by all of the students, she appeared to be adjusting well. However, one homeroom teacher, also the English teacher and a stickler for rules, proper grammar and a strict disciplinarian, chose to use our new classmate as a sample student. She ridiculed her whenever she was grammatically wrong, punished her if she didn't have all of her work done to perfection, and constantly harassed her, as if she was not worthy of respect. It wasn't long before our new classmate rebelled.

The threat of the strap, the threat of the principal being called to enforce the rules, soon catapulted into an explosive situation. One day, while being ridiculed in front of the class, our classmate got into a physical fight with our teacher. Before long, they were thrashing it out on the floor, pulling each other's hair, scratching each other, rolling and writhing about like animals. Suddenly, I could hear whispers throughout the class. A few students were trying to get the attention of the students in row one to close the door. Someone quietly tip-toed in that direction, closing it before our school principal, whose office was directly across the hall, would hear the commotion and try to stop the performance. For once, one of ours was in the running with a very good chance at winning. Without a doubt, I enjoyed class that day, even if it was but for a fleeting moment. However, occasions like these soon became the topic of boardroom discussion and a reason to implement even stricter rules. Teachers were to be respected and obeyed. After all, children, like our classmate, lacked discipline, or so said our teacher.

NUN COMES OUT OF CLOSET

The second occasion worth mentioning is very similar to the first. I may have been in Grade 10 or even Grade 11 at the time. As usual, some students were singled out more than others, almost always the girls over the boys. Girls appeared more vulnerable, no doubt, easier to make cry and easier to manipulate.

BACK OF THE POND

My friend and cousin, Theresa, who came from a strict Catholic home, was the target for our teacher that day. The subject was French and the teacher was the same nun who had strapped me earlier for not helping my brother with his French homework.

Theresa arrived at school late; upset about something, she remained in the cloakroom, at the back of the room, while the teacher waited to begin class. Frustrated with the delay, and uninterested in why my friend might have been upset, the nun walked to the back of the room and ordered her to her seat.

She then rambled on about the necessity of being on time, the inconvenience that Theresa had caused, the need to be punished. Before anyone knew what was happening, we could hear rumblings behind us. The two were fighting it out in the cloakroom, on the muddy floor among the boots, coats and accessories.

First, we could hear the throwing of things, then the knocking about as they fought each other up and down the narrow room. Unfortunately, the view was off-limits. We knew what we were in store for if we left our seats to watch. Some howls and screams later, the two emerged, my friend looking none the worst for her efforts, the nun red-faced and in disarray. They both left the classroom, returning some time later as if nothing unusual had taken place.

For the remainder of the class, as well as the remainder of the school year, my friend was never picked on again. In fact, that nun even showed a little respect in her company after that incident. I never did understand what had happened that day. I did, however, begin to recognize a Survival of the Fittest scenario. Surely life had better than that to offer.

ET TU, SISTER MARY?

My husband also had a couple of bad experiences at school. Today, he can't read without losing his breath. That would be hilarious if not for the fact that, as a young boy still in primary school, he had his head beaten up against the blackboard by his teacher, a nun; she did this because he was unable to complete his division problems.

On another occasion, he was locked in the school, and told he would be left there for the summer holidays. He believed what he was told, because he was too young to know the difference. He remembers standing on tiptoe on a chair, reaching up to a window, and watching as all the other children and teachers left the school grounds. Eventually, of course, the old hag came back and let him out.

My husband obviously had some disdain for the Catholic school he attended. As a young boy, he witnessed how his father got relief from stomach ulcers by drinking baking soda in water to make himself throw up. When he saw how well the baking soda worked for his father, Bill put this information to good use. When he wanted to stay home from school, he would sneak soda and water to his room and drink it just before his mother came to check on him. After he threw up, his mother would always send him back to bed.

By the time I graduated from high school in 1968, change was occurring very rapidly in the schools and in the homes. The baby boomer population was no longer willing to take the shut-up-and-sit-down method of teaching in rote format that had been commonplace for so long. Corporal punishment was no longer acceptable to the administration or to the parents. In fact, parents began to deal with physical punishment set down by a teacher, by taking such issues to the courtroom.

BACK OF THE POND

The last thing the school boards wanted was court cases involving their staff members. Quick changes emerged; unfortunately, in the transition, discipline problems intensified and reached a new high. For far too many children, schools began to serve more as socializing grounds, places to meet up; just somewhere to pass the days. Frustrated, overworked and stressed-out teachers got little or no support from administrators, whose loyalties lay only with those who were instrumental in advancing their positions.

Chapter 6: The Friendly Invasion

1969 marked the end of an era for me. I finally graduated from St. Stephen's High School in Stephenville. I had repeated Grade 10 and spent an extra semester in Grade 11. In January of 1969, I began a new era; the university years. Just 17 years old, I was already exhausted.

Wouldn't it be great if we could look back, keep the old memories and throw away the bad ones? We could get a fresh start, using the knowledge we gained to push us onward and upward in our new quest. We could ring out the old and ring in the new, so to speak, with no baggage, I might add, but that's not the way it goes. We take the past with us. It helps mold who we become, just as the genes that we receive from both our parents dictate our eye color, our hair color, even whether or not we will be farsighted. Can you believe that?

Our chromosomes, once we are conceived, spin out our DNA, taking into consideration a multitude of information from both our mother and our father. At this stage, we haven't consciously played any role in who we will become. From the beginning of the cycle of life, our genes determine our height, our weight, even a V-shaped hairline in some, called the widow's peak. In others, genes can determine a thumb that curves when extended, called the hitchhikers thumb. They also determine whether we have the ability to roll our tongue into a tube shape or whether or not we have freckles; of course, they also predispose so much more. I wonder which one of my parents gave me my cowlick. Even though I didn't know it at age 17, my mother's genes would come to play a huge role in what my future would be like.

My mother, Agnita LeBlanc, was born on March 15, 1919 to French-speaking parents, Tom and Julianna LeBlanc. She married my father, and they built their first home in an area they both endearingly referred to as *Back of the Pond*.

BACK OF THE POND

Back of the Pond refers specifically to the homesteads in back of Stephenville Pond, not Noel's Pond, as it is sometimes confused.

When the American Air Force Base was established on that same property in 1941, all liviers, as they were then called, were bought out and forced to move. Some moved to areas just outside Base boundaries, for example, along Blanche Brook and other pockets of land in Stephenville. My parents and both sets of grandparents moved and rebuilt on West Street. Others moved to the outskirts of Stephenville; to Kippens, the Port au Port Peninsula, St. George's, Stephenville Crossing and elsewhere. Still others moved further away to farming communities like Codroy Valley where they saw the opportunity to rebuild their lives and livelihood. One thing we must remember is that jobs came with the arrival of the American Base, so most of the liviers would have been reluctant to leave. They were deeply attached to the heart of their community; their church, their school and their friends and families.

BACK OF THE POND

It is possible that a few might have left the island, but it is very unlikely. For most, the language barrier would have been too great. The elders, especially, would have been drawn to rebuild close to those who spoke their mother tongue. The amount of money my parents were paid for their home and six chains [8] of cultivated lands would never repay the emotional and economic costs of resettlement. I was once told, "that is something, only someone who has relocated can understand."

In 1941, Newfoundland was not yet a part of Canada. It would remain under British rule for another eight years or so, after which we would join Confederation in 1949 as Canada's 10th province.

It was wartime. World War II had officially begun in 1939 and would not come to an end until 1945; because of its constitutional relationship with the United Kingdom through the commission of government, Newfoundland and Labrador had already entered into the war on September 3, 1939. The United States had made a deal with Great Britain to set up bases throughout Newfoundland in exchange for supplying Britain with 50 destroyers, and so the deal was brokered. One of those bases was established here in Stephenville.

Back of the Pond was on its way to becoming just a memory. Families that once lived on that parcel of land, wouldn't even be able to recognize the place in the years to come. They would no longer be able to point out the spot where they had once played and swam in their bare feet. Given the landscape changes the area would undergo, they wouldn't be able to find the four islands that once existed, each laid claim to by Luc Benoit (my great grandfather), James Benoit (my grandfather), Pat and Midée Gaudon and Joe Russell. They would no longer recognize the pond that teamed with large healthy fish that could be caught at short notice. They would no longer identify the places where a variety of berries grew in abundance on the islands. They would never again see wild game (like rabbit, ptarmigan, ducks, etc.) that could be trapped or hunted freely without a monetary cost.

_____

[8] Chain: a surveyor's or land chain is 66 ft. Cultivated land: land cleared for farming.

BACK OF THE POND

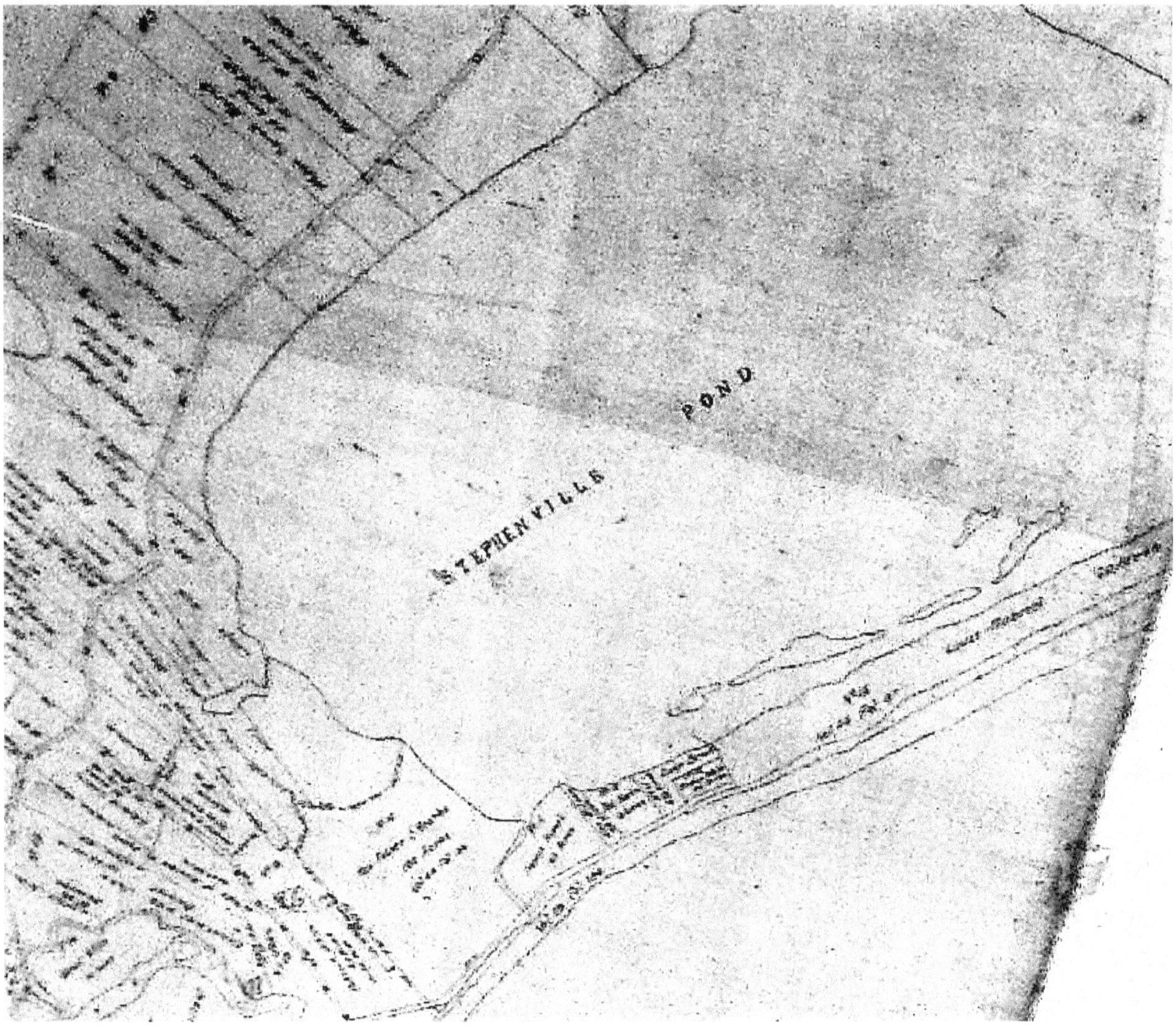

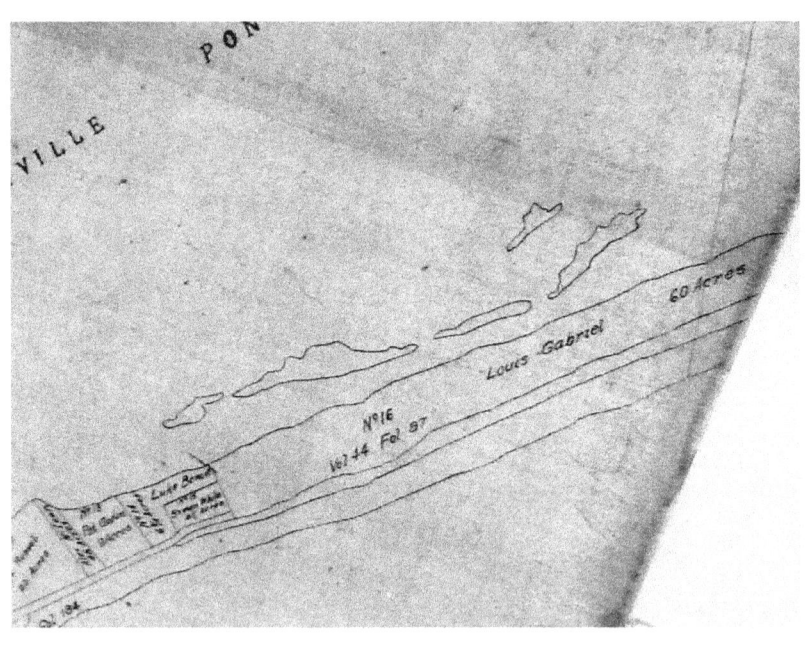

BACK OF THE POND

My father often spoke about how he felt cheated because he had left so much behind that money just couldn't buy. He often wished for that old lifestyle for all the family, and especially for his grand-children, as he saw so many losing their way. He remembered how free they were in comparison to today. They were free to fish, to hunt, to explore, to learn from their elders. Dad could easily have been called a Jack-of-all-trades; the trait he showed, time and time again, was that of patience, a trait that is sadly lacking in most children today. He often said they worked very hard, but they were happy to work and do their share. There was always something to do, which kept them busy and out of trouble.

My sister, Linda, and I drove to Little Port Harmon one day in the hopes of finding some semblance of the pond that my Dad referred to. He called it Stephenville Pond. We found a spot that my Aunt Helena (Dad's sister) had pointed out earlier as being somewhat familiar and we used this as a guide. On this day, I found a dirt road that could be entered with an all-terrain vehicle and I was able to drive the distance with my old camper van. The road ran along the pond for a kilometer or more, and looked and felt more like what Dad had described to us before his death in 2005. What was really surprising, we thought, was that we were able to pick wild peas by the handful. We immediately remembered Dad's story of how he picked peas as a child, to add to the salt beef and cabbage supper. For a few fleeting moments, I felt we were back where both our grandparents had started out in the 1800s.

Wild peas found at Little Port Harmon

BACK OF THE POND

Dad told us a number of people lived in the area and connected often. Tom LeBlanc, Mom's father, who was a well-liked man, was known for his large gatherings and parties, which they then called a "do." His house had been built where the Labrador Linerboard was erected in the '70s and where the Abitibi Paper Mill stood from 1981-2005. Dad's father, James Benoit, had built to the left of him. He said he and Mom had built their house between the two.

**The Labrador Linerboard Mill is in the background to the left.
You can also see the Stephenville Access Road (Route 490) to the far left.**

Dad described Stephenville Pond as much larger than it is today. The Islands were a two-and-a-half hour swim across the pond. They were, he said, near the beach of Bay St. George. With the coming of the American Base, the pond underwent some major changes. In the future, it had to accommodate ocean-going ships. The mountain, called Indian Head because of its resemblance to the same, was blasted, knocking off a large piece on its northern headland.

BACK OF THE POND

Indian Head viewed from Port Harmon side (2016)
Note: Indian Face and Body in the Mountain

I was told that the original "Indian Head" was plainly visible in the portion that was blasted off. If that is so, another of his tribe must have laid down and taken his place. Further blasting was done to open the channel for ships to enter the port. The pond, which was originally nine feet above sea level (according to Dad), was dredged out with large suction dredges to the depth of 25 feet. This was even more accommodating for larger vessels. Once the water level went down, the Islands were no longer surrounded by water, but instead became an extension of the land.

First, there was the building of three runways for military and commercial aircraft to come and go during the war. To make way for a larger runway, part of the pond was later filled in. How much, I don't know, but enough that liviers from the past, like my father and his family, lost sight of the way it had looked in their younger years. Today, the runways are still intact and still in use. The bigger of the two runways is much larger than most. It often receives planes that are diverted from other airports such as St. John's or Deer Lake due to fog, storms or other mishaps.

BACK OF THE POND

Stephenville Airport (YJT) boasts one of the best landing strips in Atlantic Canada and the best in Newfoundland and Labrador. Its large runway is 10,000 feet by 200 feet. Since the late 1990s, Stephenville has been designated as one of five Canadian airports suitable as an emergency landing site for the space shuttle. Changes to the Stephenville Pond with the arrival of the USAAF (United States Army Air Forces) Base to Stephenville had far more serious consequences than those mentioned above. While it reinforced the urgency of being at war, it also highlighted the bravery and honor of Newfoundlanders and Labradorians who had been, and still were, enlisting in World War II. Out of a population of 321,819 in 1945, 12,000 men and women enlisted and served abroad in one form or another. My father himself stood in line to enlist, but was told they had all the men they needed. He saw men and women, good friends of his, leave for their respective stations. The night before they left, Tom White (LeBlanc) had a "do" at his home. Everyone was there, Dad told us.

Her Majesty's ship, HMS Hood, was both the highest respected battle cruiser of the British Navy as well as its most famous warship.

HMS Hood

BACK OF THE POND

Officially, HMS Hood was never in St. George's Harbor, but in 1923, the Special Service Squadron World Cruise departed Britain for a Royal Navy Tour of the British Empire. After visiting various Empire outposts (such as India, South Africa, Australia, New Zealand and South America), they finally made their way, in the autumn of 1924, to the East Coast of Canada and to Newfoundland.

Picture of crew of HMS Hood taken September 1924
Photo courtesy of Mrs. A. Bishop, likely taken in St. George's Harbour
HMS Hood World Cruise, Special Services Squadron
Referenced by kind permission of the National Archives, London, U.K.

On the journey from Quebec City to St. John's, the cruise stopped in St. George's Harbour. The squadron consisted of the battle cruiser HMS Hood, HMAS Adelaide, and HMS Repulse. The squadron remained for several days.

BACK OF THE POND

In the harbour lived the retired Commander Cornelius Carter and Commander Victor Campbell. During their stay, the crew engaged with the locals on a soccer field, featuring the best of the Royal Navy versus the locals. The locals won 6-2. Crew members of the Australian cruiser Adelaide also competed in dory races against the locals. The Aussies held their own. On the last evening, the orchestra of the battle cruiser Hood played for the local dignitaries and the crew. Commander Carter's two daughters were guests of Captain John Thurn. The squadron then departed for St. John's.

On retirement, Captain Campbell and his wife Marit, former lady-in-waiting to Queen Maude of Norway, settled in Black Duck Siding, Newfoundland. Little did anyone know that, on her departure from St. George's Harbour, the HMS Hood would, in 18 years' time, carry the fate of three Stephenville boys: Joseph Gallant, William Gallant and Samuel Gaudet.

Sadly, on May 24, 1941, around the middle of the Second World War, the British battle cruiser HMS Hood intercepted the German Battleship Bismarck in the Battle of the Denmark Strait.

German Battleship Bismarck

BACK OF THE POND

In the North Atlantic, the Hood managed to fire off salvos, but the German Bismarck's reply was more deadly. One of the shells hit the magazine. Tons of ammunition blew up and mortally damaged the British war ship. Within minutes, the Hood had completely sunk.

Of the 1,418 crewmen aboard the Hood at the time of her sinking, only three survived. These men were Alfred Edward Briggs, Robert Ernest Tilburn and William John Dundas.

Ted Briggs was born on March 1, 1923 in Yorkshire, England. He served on the Hood from July 1939 right up until it sank. Ted was the last of the three survivors to die. He died on October 4, 2008.

Robert E. Tilburn was born in 1921 in Leeds, England. In 1938, he was drafted to the Hood. When the ship went down, Robert was working on the antiaircraft guns. Robert died in 1995.

William Dundas was born in 1925 in Perthshire, Scotland. He was posted to the Hood in 1941. William has been recognized as having kept the other two survivors awake, by singing songs, a feat that may well have saved their lives. William Dundas died in 1965.

Three of the men who went down with that ship were from Stephenville.

Left to Right: Joseph Gallant, William Gallant and Samuel Gaudet.

BACK OF THE POND

Ordinary Seaman Joseph Gallant, P/JX 212476, Royal Navy. [9] [10] Born October 27, 1919, in Stephenville, Newfoundland, he was the son of John Gallant and Elizabeth Bourgeois. A member of the Newfoundland Overseas Forestry Unit (NOFU No. 0446), he was transferred to the Navy at the start of the war. HMS Hood is believed to have been his only ship. He was a <u>first cousin of William Gallant</u> and a <u>second cousin of Samuel Gaudet</u>, both of whom were lost in the sinking. Joseph was twenty-one years old when he died.

Ordinary Seaman William Gallant, P/JX 212477, Royal Navy. [11] [12] Born June 16, 1917, in Stephenville, Newfoundland, he was the son of William and Laura Gallant. A member of the Newfoundland Overseas Forestry Unit (NOFU No. 0447), he was transferred to the Navy at the start of the war. HMS Hood is believed to have been his only ship. He was a <u>first cousin of Joseph Gallant</u> and a <u>second cousin of Samuel Gaudet</u>, both of whom were lost in the sinking. William was twenty-three years old when he died. According to relatives and friends of the family, William is remembered for having a great sense of humor.

Ordinary Seaman Samuel Gaudet, P/JX 212478, Royal Navy. [13] [14] Born August 27, 1917, in Stephenville, Newfoundland, he was the son of Octave and Mary Gaudet. A member of the Newfoundland Overseas Forestry Unit (NOFU No. 0421), he was transferred to the Navy at the start of the war. HMS Hood is believed to have been his only ship. He was a <u>second cousin to both Joseph Gallant and William Gallant</u>, both of whom were lost in the sinking. Samuel was twenty-three years old when he died.

---

[9] http://www.veterans.gc.ca/eng/remembrance/memorials/canadian-virtual-war-memorial/detail/2492741
[10] http://www.hmshood.com/crew/memorial/g/GallantJ.htm
[11] http://www.veterans.gc.ca/eng/remembrance/memorials/canadian-virtual-war-memorial/detail/2492742
[12] http://www.hmshood.com/crew/memorial/g/GallantW.htm
[13] http://www.veterans.gc.ca/eng/remembrance/memorials/canadian-virtual-war-memorial/detail/2492828
[14] http://www.hmshood.com/crew/memorial/g/GaudetS.htm

BACK OF THE POND

Dad's sister, Helena, was dating one of those Gallant boys at the time. So many, like them, performed acts of heroism to help others, and to win freedom for their allies and their country.

The following is a song called "Sink the Bismark" by Johnny Horton and Tillman Franks. It was released in 1960 by country music singer Johnny Horton. Bismarck was misspelled by the record label, an error that was corrected for later releases of the song.

The song talks about that fatal day May 24, 1941, when the British ship was sunk by the German ship Bismarck. The song avenges the lives of those lost that day, by telling of the pursuit and then the inevitable sinking of the Bismarck just three days later, on May 27, 1941. Unfortunately, there is yet another error in the lyrics, and that is the falsehood that the sinking of the Bismarck took seven days, when it indeed only took three days after the sinking of the Hood.

In May of 1941 the war had just begun
The Germans had the biggest ship that had the biggest guns
The Bismark was the fastest ship that ever sailed the seas
On her deck were guns as big as steers and shells as big as trees

Out of the cold and foggy night came the British ship the Hood
And every British seaman, he knew and understood
They had to sink the Bismark, the terror of the sea
Stop those guns as big as steers and those shells as big as trees

We'll find that German battleship that's makin' such a fuss
We gotta sink the Bismark 'cause the world depends on us
Hit the decks a-runnin' boys and spin those guns around
When we find the Bismark we gotta cut her down

The Hood found the Bismark and on that fatal day
The Bismark started firin' fifteen miles away

BACK OF THE POND

We gotta sink the Bismark was the battle sound
But when the smoke had cleared away, the mighty Hood went down

For six long days and weary nights they tried to find her trail
Churchill told the people, "Put ev'ry ship a-sail"
'Cause somewhere on that ocean I know she's gotta be
We gotta sink the Bismark to the bottom of the sea

We'll find that German battleship that's makin' such a fuss
We gotta sink the Bismark 'cause the world depends on us
Hit the decks a-runnin' boys and spin those guns around
When we find the Bismark we gotta cut her down

The fog was gone on the seventh day and they saw the mornin' sun
Ten hours away from homeland the Bismark made its run
The admiral of the British fleet said, "Turn those bows around"
We found that German battleship and we're gonna cut her down

The British guns were aimed and the shells were comin' fast
The first shell hit the Bismark, they knew she couldn't last
That mighty German battleship is just a memory
"Sink the Bismark", was the battle cry that shook the seven seas

We found that German battleship was makin' such a fuss
We had to sink the Bismark 'cause the world depends on us
We hit the decks a-runnin' and we spun those guns around
Yeah, we found the mighty Bismark and then we cut her down

We found that German battleship was makin' such a fuss
We had to sink the Bismark 'cause the world depends on us
We hit the decks a-runnin' and we spun those guns around
We found the mighty Bismark and then we cut her down

This song is in the public domain, but certain settings, performances and recordings may still be protected.

THE BABY BOOMER AGE

Following the end of World War II and the return of the young men and women to their homelands, there was a renewed sense of hope. With new innovations and technology on the rise, this resulted in an era of prosperity; thus came the increase in pregnancies, the greater number between 1946 and 1964. Baby boomers are the demographic group born during those post-war years. They would be approximately between the ages of 52 and 70 in the year 2016. I was born in 1951, and I recently turned 65. I, therefore, am a baby boomer.

During the war, President Franklin D. Roosevelt was very concerned about the morale of American soldiers. He brought together, among other organizations, an entertainment division called the U.S.O. (United Service Organization) to lift the spirits of American troops and their families. When the American base was still active in Stephenville (and before its closure in 1966), celebrities and singers like Bob Hope, Marilyn Monroe, Frank Sinatra, Jayne Mansfield and others came to Stephenville to entertain the GI's (Private Soldiers in the U.S. Army).

On one occasion, the featured performer was Kitty Wells, and one of her guests was Johnny Cash. When Kitty went to introduce Johnny, she realized he was late. She ended up apologizing for his absence a number of times. Finally, Johnny arrived. He, of course, excused himself for not being on time. He said he had run into an old friend, an officer, who was now Captain at Stephenville base. The crowd was grateful to see him and soon forgave his tardiness, and the show went on. It was later discovered that Mr. Cash had indeed met up with an old buddy. It seems that he had bumped into a gentleman by the name of Basil Cormier, who then invited him to his home in Kippens for a drink. Once there, out came Captain Morgan, and the rest, my friends, is history.

BACK OF THE POND

This might be a good time to reminisce, once more, about the quiet Acadian community *Back of the Pond* and one among them who was thought to be eccentric because of his prophesies. It was discovered, however, that his visions into the future would eventually prove to be well-founded. This elderly gentleman would, on occasion, imagine (or foresee) events that were foreign to the others. The local population thought him somewhat *off-center, and held some doubt about his intentions to make sense* (a common saying among the Acadian families).

Marcella LeBlanc was an Acadian farmer. A married man with no children, he was well respected in the town for his work ethic. Nevertheless, he sometimes left his neighbors wondering. In his limited vocabulary, he would describe unusual events as he envisioned them.

He saw flying metal objects that he called flying kettles (because that was the best way he knew how to describe an airplane). On another occasion, he asked his neighbors if they had seen the large ship in Stephenville Pond; a strange thing to say, considering that Stephenville Pond didn't become a harbor until the 1950s. There was excitement in Marcella's voice when he reported to his friends that, while hauling a load of wood with his horses, he had to put the team of horses into the woods in order to avoid an oncoming train. It wasn't until the 1940s that the aircraft arrived in Newfoundland and a rail line was constructed. After the Stephenville Pond was dredged in the 1950s, the ships could then enter the harbor.

Marcella's remarkable foresight extended beyond modes of transportation. He envisioned that one day, people would go inside their homes to use their toilets, and lo and behold, they would go outside their homes to eat their meals. Ironically, Marcella's sense of insight failed him when he couldn't remember where he had hidden his money. There was no bank back then. His neighbor, Mr. Vincent Cormier, helped him find it. It was under a wood stump.

BACK OF THE POND

Another part of our history, and an influence that cannot be ignored, is Sandy Point.

Sandy Point is an island, formerly a peninsula, in Bay St. George, Newfoundland, which was thought to be inhabited by Aboriginal peoples such as the Dorset, Eskimo and later the Beothuk and Mi'kmaq nations. They were eventually followed by a variety of British and European peoples.

Sandy Point was often called a hidden island because of the difficulty of spotting it on the horizon when approaching the inner bay from the Gulf of St. Lawrence. This feature was beneficial to pirate vessels and thieves; it made Sandy Point a temporary hiding place from regular trade routes in the Gulf of St. Lawrence. Since the fur trade was so lucrative at that time, the Inner Bay may also have served as a hideaway from the authorities.

Lewis Hill
815 m.
Long Point
Broad Cove
Black Duck
Brook
Winterhouse
Fox Island
River
Fox
Lourdes
Tea Cove
Port au Port Bay
Point
au Mal
Salmon Cove
Three Rock Cove
Point au Mal
West Bay
East Bay
Spruce Brook
Georges Lake
Gallants
Hare H
596 m
West Bay Centre
Cold Brook
Mainland
PORT AU PORT
PENINSULA
Red Island
Cape Cormorant
Boswarlos
Port au Port
Stephenville
Black Duck
Marches
Point
Abrahams Cove
Aguathuna
Red Brook
Petit Jardin
Cape St. George
Cape St. George
Grand Jardin
De Grau
Sheaves Cove
Lower Cove
Ship Cove
Jerrys Nose
Campbells Creek
Felix Cove
Bellmans Cove
Berry Head
Romaines
Kippens
Noels Pond
Stephenville
Crossing
Mattis
Point
Southwest
Barachois Pond
Seal Rocks
Barachois Brook
Shallop Cove
St. George's
Flat Bay
Steel Mountain
306 m.
St. George's Bay
St. Teresa
Dennis
Pond
555 m
Fischells
Heatherton
Mount Howley
453 m.
596 m.
Robinsons
McKays
Jeffreys
Cartyville
Portage Lake

Stephenville
Crossing
461
Mattis Point
461
490
Barachois
Brook
1
Saint George's

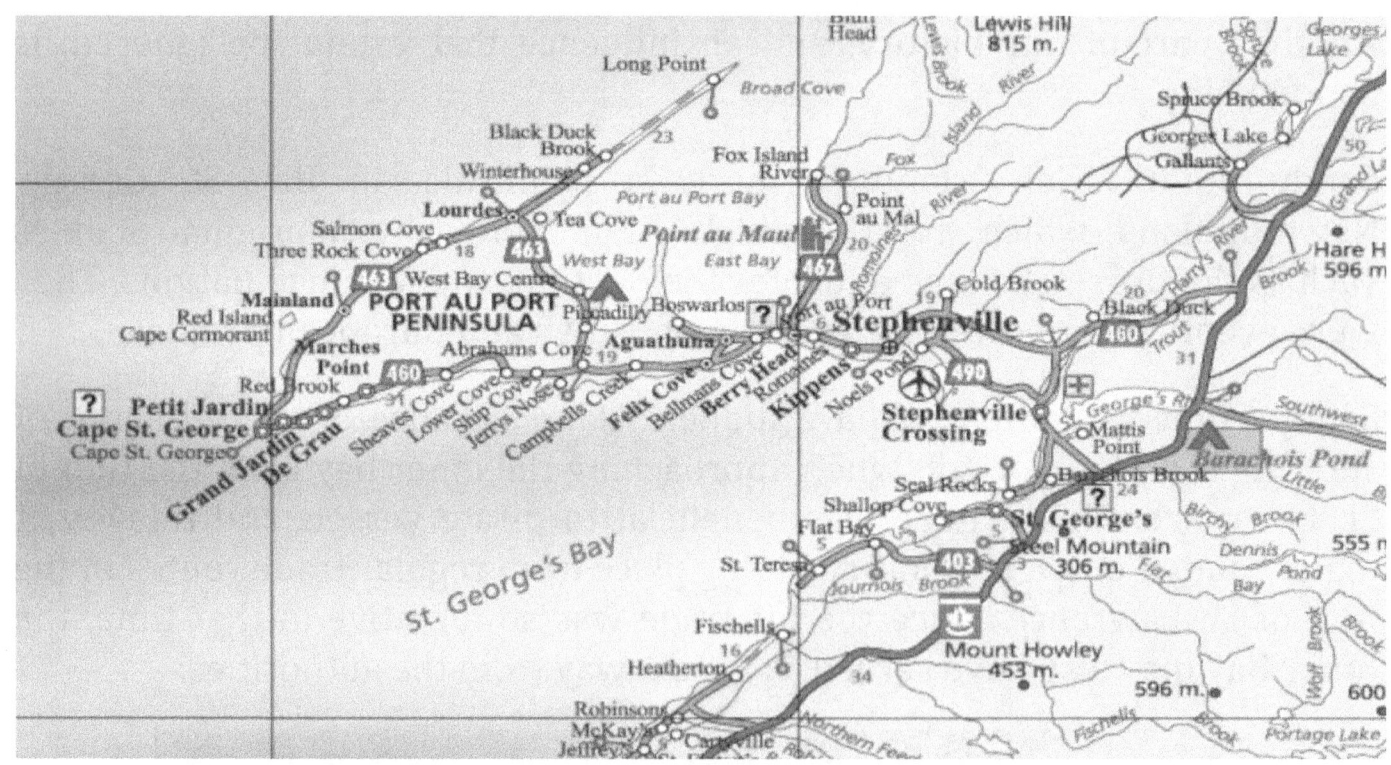

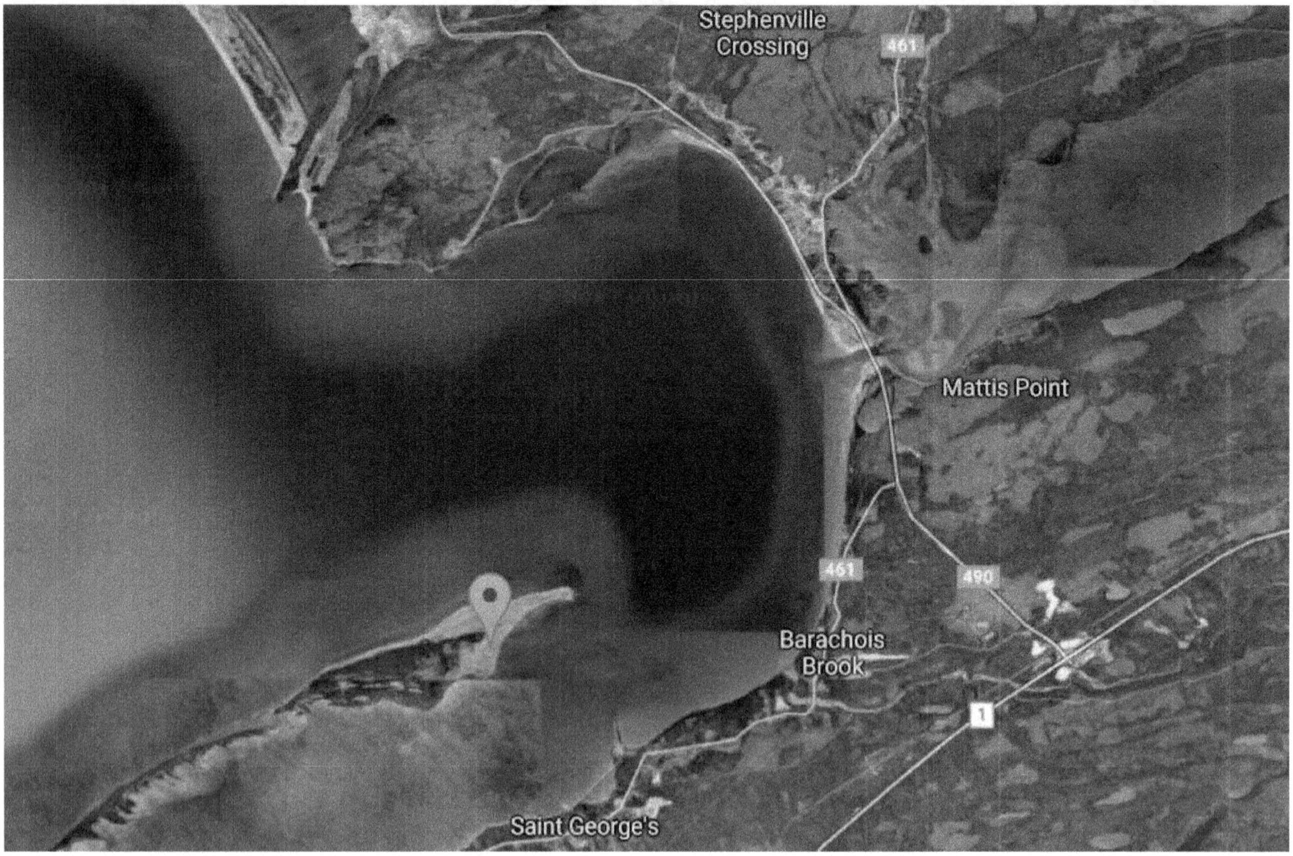

BACK OF THE POND

Sandy Point (1949) © Artist Lloyd Pretty
Reprinted here with permission

Sandy Point's natural harbour began to attract fishermen from all over. Eventually, as the peninsula became inhabited, the settlers began to coin names for their favorite fishing banks, such as "The Black Scrape," "Fanny's Crack," "Messervey's Point" and "Doubloon Bank." The latter gives rise to a story about a local fisherman jigging a fish, taking it home, and after gutting it, finding a Spanish coin called a doubloon. This gave some credibility to the likelihood that pirates and Basque whalers had previously been familiar with the area.

Later, during the construction of the Stephenville Air Base runways, while excavating near the beach, the workers discovered a chest that was still intact. The chest was removed and handed over to the Base Commander and the authorities. Days later, the men noted that a different Commander was in place; the chest was never heard of again. This story was told to me by my father, Patrick Benoit, who witnessed the event while working on the runway. To add to the intrigue of this tale, let's go back to the 1930s.

Marjorie Carter, a young resident of Barachois Brook, had a favorite spot to practice her diving skills. It was a small, deep pond in a grove of woods, near the mouth of the river. She was eventually proficient enough to be able to dive to the bottom of the pond.

BACK OF THE POND

On one of those dives, she happened to feel some sort of crate or box on the bottom. She told her story to her friends, but there was no attempt to recover the container. While this doesn't prove that the container held any treasures, it definitely piques one's interest in the possibilities, further contributing to the folklore of the Inner Bay.

Another possible reason for Spanish coins being found in the area was the foundering of two Basque whalers in about 1591. In 1594, the Bristol ship *Grace* arrived, near what is commonly called "The Gut." On shore, they observed a number of Aboriginals. By the time some of the crew made it to shore, the Natives had fled. The crew estimated that there had been approximately fifty men, women and children in that group. They also found a number of camps that indicated that these Aboriginals had been in the area for some time. They surmised that the reason for their stay may have been the attraction of the steel and iron from those abandoned ships (i.e., anchors, nails, etc.). These were two wrecked Basque whalers whose crew almost undoubtedly carried coins. Here was another huge possibility for the folklore tale of the doubloon to be true.

Eric Cobham (from Poole, England) and his wife, Maria Lindsey (from Plymouth, England) practiced piracy in the Gulf of St. Lawrence from their base on Sandy Point, Bay St. George (south-west coast of Newfoundland) for the better part of twenty years (1720-1740). Preying mostly on French ships, they became known for giving "no quarter," meaning all the captured crews were killed and the ships sunk to ensure there were no witnesses. They were famous for their cruelty and sadism, often using survivors for target practice.

Having evaded capture for two decades, they eventually set sail for France where they sold their fleet of ships (and cargo) and bought a fine estate near Le Havre. Having secured a place among the landed gentry of French society, Eric Cobham reinvented himself as a wealthy landowner and a pillar of respectability. He became a magistrate and then a judge. Unable to make the adjustment, Maria became reclusive; it is stated that she may have gone insane, possibly committing suicide.

BACK OF THE POND

Not long thereafter, Eric had an attack of conscience. Before he died, he confessed to a priest (about their life of piracy and murder); he also requested that the true story of his life be published. Survived by two sons and a daughter, they were horrified and stunned to learn that their apparently respectable parents had been a pair of ruthless buccaneers.

In an attempt to suppress the book, it is said that they bought up every copy and had them burned; however, one fragmentary, first draft, copy is said to have found its way into the Archives Nationales in Paris, where it has remained hidden from view for the past century.

Chapter 7: Life's Challenges

Having moved inside the Stephenville boundaries, my parents built this house.

Identical to the one they had to leave behind, it was located at 30 West Street. They had a family of four boys and four girls.

What I remember of my mother was that she was frail, small in stature and very soft-spoken. She was a very quiet person, pensive even; because she was anemic, probably all of her life, she didn't have the energy to keep up with the tasks of caring for her large family.

Mom kept her thoughts away from us children. Those thoughts, though, she definitely shared with Dad. They were very close. He thought the world of Mom and it showed in all he did for her, up until the day we buried her. He baked, he sewed, he cooked, and he kept us in line. He did everything he could to help her around the house. Many friends (particularly the children of Gerald and Jean Benoit as well as the children of Omar and Rita Gaudon) told me about how their parents and ours, with all children in tow, would go to the beach or the country on many occasions to get Mom away from the house, due to her lingering bouts of depression.

My parents were very secretive about their life. I don't ever remember it mentioned that Mom wasn't feeling well, or that we should be extra quiet.

BACK OF THE POND

I can remember though, doing the wash, the cleaning, even painting walls, at a very early age. I wasn't asked or told to do it. I just took that interest in the house. Maybe deep down I knew that all was not right. I felt bad for Mom because she looked so frail.

My parents were also secretive about life in the community, about gossip, about sex, and especially about religion. No discussion ever took place on those matters. It was more like "you followed the rules as the church handed them down." Mom, at least, saw no need to contemplate further. We all knew she had the final say, and Dad was volunteered to see that the rules were followed. In Mom's eyes, to question was to disbelieve, especially when it came to matters of the church.

To give you some idea of just how ingrained the Catholic religion was in our lives, I'd like to show you the birthday present I received on my fifteenth birthday.

It was a framed picture of the Blessed Virgin Mary, given to me by my friends. Someone wrote all the names on the back of the picture, along with the inscription by Walter March. I must have known there was a good reason to keep such an item after all these years.

BACK OF THE POND

The glass and frame has long been broken and thrown out. I don't know why, but I just didn't have the heart to throw the picture out. It is so precious. Nostalgic, I guess, is the correct word to describe it.

A devout Catholic, someone once told me that Mom was president of St. Anne's Guild in her final years. She followed all the rules such as church attendance on Sunday and rosary every evening, if possible. It seemed she had a knack for starting the rosary in the middle of our favorite television program, "The Beverly Hillbillies."

Taken in front of the old Roman Catholic School Circa early 1930's

My mother, Agnita White (LeBlanc), who was born in 1919, is in the third row from the front. She might have been around thirteen. The less confusing way to identify her is to count eleven girls left of the nuns. The only other person on the picture that I can name is Monsignor Adams, located in the back on the left.

Taken in front of the old Roman Catholic School Circa early 1930's

We lived in a lane, now called James Street, after my grandfather, James Benoit, who lived across West Street from us. It was all the property of my grandfather before he sold it to his children. In that lane, there were three families of Benoit's: three brothers and their families, a total of 29 children.

It was common, hard luck at the time, we thought, to say the rosary at home, and then to get caught in a second recital only minutes later. After the beads were completed at our house, it was only normal that we, especially the boys, beat it for Uncle Joe's, wanting our cousins to come out to play. Sometimes, that knock on their door was followed by an invitation to kneel with them, while they finished their rosary. Once we had knocked, there was no getting away. They didn't take 'no' for an answer.

BACK OF THE POND

I can still hear the speeded-up version of the Hail Mary, said hastily by Uncle Joe's boys. It was hilarious to us, and difficult to understand, but Joe always liked things done expediently, didn't he? If you had the occasion to meet Joe in his younger days, you would know what I mean.

I can also recall the image of Nina, my eldest sister, as the rosary was being said. She would have a chair placed in front of her, partially kneeling, and one knee on the chair, so as not to disturb the crease she had just pressed into her pants. I can recall her anxiously waiting for her date to pick her up following the rosary recital.

As children, we were always protected from whatever was going on around us. Secrets were whispered. French was deliberately spoken so we would not understand what was said. French was not shared with us, as children, because Mom and Dad were afraid we would be punished in school for speaking it, just as they had been when they were children.

I can picture Dad standing in the small hallway, where the one phone hung on the wall, having conversations, partly in French, partly in English. The two languages would automatically overlap, as some words are the same, or close, in pronunciation. Dad spoke loudly, so it wasn't difficult to pick up pieces of the conversation. If we heard our names spoken, as we sometimes did, our ears would prick up a little. Sometimes we were able to pick out the gist of the message being relayed. Still, almost every piece of news was guarded, if possible, from reaching our ears. News was hush-hush, to our detriment sometimes, no doubt, like the story of my older sister, Linda, being raised by our grandparents. The following two stories may give you an idea of just how secretive they could be.

When our next-door neighbor had a miscarriage one evening, I witnessed the screeching sound of tires and rocks flying, as someone went frantically for the priest. I got a phone call from my mother, who had gone next door to help. Obviously upset and alarmed, she asked if I could call my father from his job as a fireman on West Street. When I asked what was wrong, I was told, "Oh nothing, everything is fine, just tell your father to come home."

BACK OF THE POND

Pregnancies were hidden, if possible, and never discussed. Pregnancy and sex were embarrassing topics that rarely, if ever, got mentioned at home.

Another somewhat similar event took place in our family home while I was still in high school. My mother wasn't well, which was a very common occurrence. Her bedroom was off the kitchen and I knew that she was very sick, because her door was kept closed. Also, my father was going to and from their bedroom to the bathroom, showing obvious signs of distress. Our bathroom was not off the bedroom as many are today. I asked several times if I could help and if there was any reason for concern. As usual I was told that all was fine, but I knew better. The only thing he would ask of me was that I run quickly to McLennon's store on West Street to buy some sanitary products. Later, I realized that she had been hemorrhaging badly, and later yet, I would learn that she had cancer.

It was June 1972. I had completed my semester at university, after which I had to have a medical procedure performed at St. Clare's Mercy Hospital. I was released from the hospital just in time to celebrate my 21st birthday on June 6. My friends took me out to celebrate. I returned home to Stephenville, the next day, on June 7.

My brother, Vernon, picked me up at Stephenville Airport. Only then did I realize how dire Mom's condition was. No one had dared give me bad news while I was in school or while I had surgery to contend with. Once again, I would learn for myself how sick my mother really was, and that she wasn't going to be with us much longer. Dad nursed her at home where she wanted to be. He lifted and carried her whenever it was necessary for her to be moved. He stayed with her constantly, losing precious hours of sleep, which would take its toll on him later. On June 21, just two weeks after returning home, I travelled in the ambulance with my mother to the hospital. When we arrived there, she asked the nurses who I was. She couldn't even recognize her own daughter. Mom slipped into a coma shortly after we reached the hospital. Finally, we convinced Dad to get some badly needed sleep. Linda and I took a shift that night. When I couldn't keep my eyes open any longer, she convinced me to lie down for a short nap. I had just laid down when she woke me up to tell me Mom had died.

BACK OF THE POND

Dad, as always, had carried out Mom's last wishes. He had kept the bad news about her condition to himself. Once again, I knew that was the way she wanted it. That was the way our parents, and most other parents, dealt with tragedy. We were sheltered from the news, as if by keeping the bad news away, it wouldn't harm us.

Mom placed so much value on education. She hadn't allowed her illness to get in the way of my schooling or my exams. Little did she know that I had issues of my own that were interfering with my grades. While, on the one hand, I was able to accomplish 100 per cent on a university Math course (which I should have framed), on the other hand, I didn't realize that I had done the same Psychology course twice.

I had always felt a lack of guidance in the transition between high school and university. I was still experiencing those same feelings of light-headedness, fuzzy slow thinking, headaches and memory problems that I'd had throughout my life. I had no extracurricular activities or hobbies to balance my day or ensure a healthier lifestyle. I still didn't realize what was wrong. My only recourse was to study more, try harder, never give up and therefore, ultimately, overcome.

I now feel that I suffered a breakdown while in university; at the time, however, I thought that was normal, and in some bizarre way, I thought that was not necessarily a bad thing. The Catholic Church had always taught me that suffering, in whatever form, was a virtue, one that would allow me to accumulate rungs on the stairway to heaven. Whoa ... was my mind in trouble. The Bible can elaborate: "Just as the patriarch Jacob in the Old Testament story dreamed of a ladder which reached to heaven, there are more rungs to climb on the suffering ladder, all the way to God's glorious presence." [15]

---

[15] Climbing Jacobs Ladder: Understanding Suffering by Leona Choy. This blog entry is dated Sunday, March 27, 2011, and can be viewed at http://leonachoy.blogspot.ca/2011/03/climbing-jacobs-ladderunderstanding.html

BACK OF THE POND

The Catholic Church teaches, along with the apostles and Christians since the time of Jesus, that there is intrinsic spiritual value in suffering. The scriptures don't teach that God causes suffering, but that he sometimes permits it for his divine purposes.

After the funeral, my father collapsed at the gravesite. He had suffered a heart attack and would spend the next few weeks in hospital. It would take Dad years to recover from losing Mom. It was over those years that I learned about my mother, her illness, her depression.

Lack of sleep tormented my father. He couldn't sleep without getting the hag. I've had the unfortunate opportunity to experience the hag myself, so I knew how dreadful it felt. The night hag is a form of sleep paralysis. Folklore used a fantasy creature to explain the phenomenon of the presence of a supernatural, malevolent being, that was able to immobilize a person, as if he or she was sitting on their chest or at the foot of their bed.

Dad described it as a feeling of paralysis while something (maybe even your own hands) is reaching up to choke you. The hag was accompanied by a nightmarish, horrifying feeling unlike any other. While he was in the hag, he would scream out in terror until my husband or I would shake him, or call him out of the paralysis.

After Mom's passing, our siblings went their separate ways.

From 15-year-old Larry to 30-year-old Nina, all eight children branched out in eight different directions. After I got married in 1975, at age 24, my Dad came to live with me and my husband in Aguathuna, Port au Port West. He remained with us for 17 years. He later rented an apartment in Stephenville, for a few years, before he retired to the seniors' home in Stephenville Crossing, of his own accord, I might add. He always insisted he didn't want to become a burden on his family.

It was such a traumatic and final leap from the family home with Mom in it, to that empty house with all stability gone, that nothing was the same again. When we lost Mom, we lost contact with most of her family connections.

BACK OF THE POND

We got tidbits of information from time to time, like the fact that she was related to people from Cold Brook. We learned that she had a sister, Molly, who had died when she was just 33 years old, while giving birth to a daughter, Mary. We heard that she had two sisters who died as children, Viola and Mercedes, and that maybe I was named after Mercedes. We also heard rumors that there was one more sibling, but we don't have the statistics to prove it.

Believe me; it took years and years to connect so many dots when we were not told those things at a young age. We now have grandchildren of our own, yet many of our family members know very little about the White (LeBlanc) side. Linda does, because she has made it a hobby to work on the family tree, and so does Nina, because she was the oldest and had more access to Mom's extended family, because of the extra years she spent with her.

So many years were stolen from us: years when we could have gotten to know each other better; years when we could have bonded; not child to mother, so much as adult to adult.

When Mom passed away on June 22, 1972, her only living sibling was her brother, Roddie White (LeBlanc), married to Angie Hynes. Most of our family had a close connection to Uncle Roddie's family. We also had close ties with Uncle Austin's family (married to Mercedes McIsaac), even though Austin, had died at the early age of 49, twelve years before Mom's death.

Many other family links are a tangled web, especially for younger members of our family. It makes me wonder as to the possible truth of the Walter Scott quote: *O, what a tangled web we weave when first we practice to deceive!*

BACK OF THE POND

In the centre is Julianna White (LeBlanc). Standing in the background is her daughter, Molly. Her son, Roddie is on her left; her son, Austin is on her right. In front is her daughter, Mercedes.

BACK OF THE POND

With the loss of my mother, I feel I've lost a goodly portion of my identity, much in the same way a woman loses her identity when she takes on her husband's surname and drops her own. When I married, of course, the normal thing to do was to assume his name and drop mine. Today, I realize, many women opt to keep their name and add their husband's surname to theirs. Similarly, because my maiden name is Benoit, I don't identify with the White's (Leblanc's) in a group or at a function; thus, there was always a measure of distance kept between me and my mother's people (not deliberately, I realize).

That distancing changed the dynamics of who I would become, the direction I would travel, in some sense. However, there was one dynamic that the course of time and events had little bearing on and that was DNA, specifically my mother's. I learned, through information acquired via different sources, that my mother, from a very young age, dealt with extreme depression. Having to be hospitalized numerous times, she was most vulnerable around the time of her first pregnancies. Being as religious as she was, she certainly would have adhered to the Catholic Church's ruling that birth control, in any form, was not permitted. She had her first two pregnancies just 11 months apart, which left her unable to cope, at a time when her babies needed her most. Over the next 13 to 14 years, she would have six more children. In that weakened state, she would have been vulnerable to disease, and so it wasn't surprising that cancer set in.

Mom had only 31 years between her first pregnancy and her death. Within those 31 years, she had eight children; coupled within those pregnancies, she lived with her stages of cancer. Since she died so young, at the age of fifty-three, we have little information about her. Due to the fact that my mother insisted on keeping personal health problems from us, we might never know whether or not she miscarried. Pregnancies were common because birth control was condemned by the church. Her already weakened state during her child-bearing years makes it very likely that she did have at least a miscarriage or two.

BACK OF THE POND

When my mother died in 1972, we had never heard of the Allderdice Syndrome, named after Dr. Penny W. Allderdice, nor did we have any knowledge of chromosomes and how they would play a part in our family's history, in such a short time. Genetic studies on chromosomes were in their early stages back then; in fact, it wasn't until 1956 that it became genetically accepted that the karyotype of man included 23 pairs, or 46 chromosomes.[16]

As a result of the research of Dr. Allderdice and others, a breakthrough was made in the discovery of an irregular chromosome within the LeBlanc family line. This irregularity had, for generations, been responsible for multiple, congenital abnormities, and/or deaths in infants. With this knowledge, doctors can now better inform and treat affected families, in a much more meaningful way.

---

[16] https://en.wikipedia.org/wiki/Cytogenetics

Chapter 8: Allderdice Syndrome

Étienne LeBlanc and Anne Marie Cormier were married on June 23, 1817 at St. Michael's Parish in Margaree, Inverness County, Nova Scotia. [17] [18] This Acadian couple passed down a gene defect to their offspring. Having moved to Sandy Point in Bay St. George, a pioneering community and commercial centre on the west coast of Newfoundland, both had an identical genetic defect in their genes, the combination of which we all know today as the Allderdice Syndrome. As more members of the LeBlanc family married and relocated, the condition became so far-reaching that it was no longer contained to the LeBlanc surname.

In the past two centuries there have been hundreds of babies, who either died during their nine months of development within the womb or shortly thereafter. In the 1970s, one doctor in particular, with the help of other doctors in the field, took a special interest in identifying common traits among those babies; multiple abnormalities that proved to be genetically linked, and showed up in as many as six generations.

To get to this common link or thread, Dr. Penny W. Allderdice had meticulously documented pedigree data from families who had been affected by the disease. The information she gathered was then followed up by a blood test called a "karyotype of the blood," which tested whether or not one carried an affected third chromosome. That information, coupled with searches of marriage records, baptismal and death records from 1812-1845, resulted in identifying an inversion 3 chromosome irregularity, one with far-reaching effects.

---

[17] https://www.wikitree.com/wiki/Leblanc-1120
https://www.wikitree.com/genealogy/Leblanc-Family-Tree-1120
[18] https://www.wikitree.com/wiki/Cormier-359
https://www.wikitree.com/genealogy/Cormier-Family-Tree-359

BACK OF THE POND

Today, in 2016, for instance, we have more recent developments in gene editing and chromosome banding techniques. For example, using less than 1 per cent of a donor's DNA, scientists have found a way to prevent a number of children from inheriting potentially fatal diseases from their parents. [19] Research continues to be ongoing. Since the Allderdice Syndrome was first discovered in the 1970s, there have been many breakthroughs. Over 45 years have passed; such developments, as the one mentioned above, will give hope to many families and will continue, no doubt, to bring comfort to many more mothers in the future. More recently, additional carriers and affected infants have been reported from Canada, France and Russia. This condition has become far reaching, beyond western Newfoundland, and is no longer contained to one surname.

Genetic research at the MUN Faculty of Medicine began with the appointment in 1975 of cytogeneticist Dr. Penny Allderdice. It was she who discovered a link in the family tree of the early LeBlanc family. It appears that some individuals carry a re-arrangement of their chromosomes, meaning all genetic material is present, but not in the correct order. Our specific arrangement, as Dr. Allderdice noted, is an inversion of chromosome 3. A chromosome, with an inversion, contains a piece that has been broken off, flipped around 180 degrees and reinserted.

In 2008, I was tested for the Allderdice Syndrome, but luckily my test was negative. Had I tested positive, I would have had a 40 percent chance of having a child with missing or extra chromosome 3 material, born with mental or physical defects. Of course, you must realize that this information, if positive, would have been too late for me, but *not* too late for my children and grandchildren.

---

[19] The Western Star, Weekend Edition – December 24, 2016 article entitled *Big Leaps in Gene Editing Raise Ethical Questions About Human Application* retrieved from
https://www.npr.org/2016/12/24/506817063/big-leaps-in-gene-editing-raise-ethical-questions-about-human-application

BACK OF THE POND

An inversion 3 carrier can pass on his or her chromosomes in four different ways, resulting in [1] a healthy child, with perfectly normal chromosomes, [2] a healthy child, who is an inversion carrier, [3] a child with missing or extra chromosome 3 material that miscarries during the pregnancy, [4] a child with missing or extra chromosome 3 material born with mental and/or physical disabilities.

Every time an inversion carrier has a child, there can be as high as a two in five chance of having a child born with serious medical problems.

With a look back at my grandmother, Julianna LeBlanc (Mom's mother) and her offspring, a history of health problems once again emerges. Only now, in my senior years, have I learned that my grandmother only lived to be forty-five years old. My older sister remembers being told that when my grandmother visited *Back of the Pond*, she would immediately be given a comfortable chair and seated as close to the door as possible, so she could get fresh air. Just like my mother, she, too, was very frail and anemic.

When Julianna passed away, my mother, Agnita, was just seven years old. At this early age, she would have been the only female in her father's household, with her father and two older brothers, Austin (15) and Roddie (13). Her older sister, Molly, was just starting her own family with her husband, Columbus White; they had their first child, Myron, just a year earlier. The death of my grandmother, Julianna, would surely have been a difficult time for my mother. It might have also brought her closer to her sister, Molly.

Molly now had the extra task of transitioning my mother through childhood into adulthood. In many ways she had to take on the role of mother, as well as big sister. Even though their close bonding was a good thing, it once again placed my mother in a very vulnerable position.

Unexpectedly, some fourteen years later, Tom LeBlanc, Mom's father, took sick and died. Mom was now twenty-one years old. His death was very stressful on the family.

BACK OF THE POND

I've been told by many that Tom was a very sociable and charismatic character; he was the life of a party, the life of the community, and the life of his family. At the time of his death he was sixty-two years old. Molly was remembered by some as mourning his loss by crying and uttering aloud the words "everyone is dying." They had also just lost their beloved family horse.

To add to the sorrow of this family, just months later, in the same year, Molly tragically died, at the early age of thirty-three, while giving birth to her daughter, Mary, (now Mary O'Quinn). Left to mourn her were eight children, ages birth to fifteen years, her husband Columbus, her two brothers, Austin and Roddie, and her only sister, Agnita, my mother. My mother's resolve must surely have been shaken, for good, this time. It's no wonder she suffered a nervous breakdown in the upcoming months.

With the death of her sister, roles were suddenly reversed. It was now time for my mother to be there for her nieces and nephews: Mary (newborn); Clifton (twenty-two months); Mercedes (three years); Genevieve (five years); Wilfred (ten years); Pauline (twelve years); Edna (thirteen years); and Myron (fifteen years old). They were all very close to one another, as close as any family could possibly be. One beautiful memory that Wilfred held onto, was that my mother used to make donuts, and he would cry if he didn't get to eat the hole.

In summary, my mother lost at least two sisters, maybe more siblings; she lost her mother when she was seven; she lost her father when she was twenty-one, and her sister, Molly, died at the age of thirty-three, just months after their father passed away.

Within a year, at the age of twenty-two, my mother married my father, Patrick (Benoit) and they immediately started their family of eight children. This cycle of child bearing threw her into postpartum depression, which was followed by a series of health problems. Those problems, obviously hereditary, ended her life at the early age of fifty-three.

BACK OF THE POND

Medical professionals agree that mental health and physical health go hand-in-hand. I don't think I'm far off in surmising that my grandmother experienced symptoms of depression, just like my mother and me. Regardless of whether or not Mom was personally affected by Allderdice Syndrome, it has proven true, by research, that her mother was a carrier; likewise for her sister, Molly, and her brother Roddie. With such a family history, I feel a dire need to put this information forward to all Acadian families, regardless of surname, in the event that it may save someone some undue distress or pain in the future.

Over the past 50 years or so, I've had a number of close relatives deal with the stress and hardship of losing a child through this chromosome irregularity. The following two letters were written by two of my cousins who dealt with such a loss. They, too, want to share their stories with you.

LETTER # 1

My name is Mercedes (White/LeBlanc) Stevenson. I was born and raised in Stephenville, Newfoundland. I was married in 1963, and moved to Cranston, RI, USA where I still reside. On October 4, 1971, after a full-term pregnancy, I gave birth to a beautiful baby boy who weighed approximately seven pounds. Shortly after delivery, I was approached by my gynecologist who sadly had to tell me that my baby had multiple congenital abnormalities and that he was not expected to live. He lived for ten days.

The unexpected death of our baby boy after a very normal nine month pregnancy came as a shock to our family, so when we were approached by our pediatrician as to whether we would agree to an autopsy, we gave our permission.

I received a telephone call from Dr. Penny Allderdice during the summer of 1973. At that time, she was very active in her study of similar childhood abnormalities afflicting the children born to parents living on the west coast of Newfoundland. Her study of the Inverted Chromosome 3 resulted in what is now known as the "Allderdice Syndrome."

At the time of her visit, my family and I were tested for the Inverted Chromosome. I tested positive as a carrier and so did two of my three children.

My sister Edna (White/LeBlanc) Brophy, was living with me at the time of the doctor's visit. Edna is a carrier and also two of her three children. Her daughter, Jena Archer, wrote a letter (which will follow the autopsy information here) *telling of her experience while pregnant with her fourth child. Jena also miscarried two earlier pregnancies.*

The following is the autopsy report for my child as presented by the geneticist.

Case 5 100471, V1-44 Genetic Findings and Autopsy

The chromosome count of case 5 was 46. His mother, V-63, is an inv(3) p25q21 carrier; his father's karyotype is normal, 46, xy. He was the product of the fifth pregnancy of 34-year old parents: the first pregnancy ended in a spontaneous miscarriage; the next three were normal.

He was delivered at 39 weeks gestation. The APGAR score was 2 at 1 minute and 5 at 5 minutes. His condition was poor and he needed intra-tracheal oxygen under pressure. Respiratory distress persisted, and the heart was enlarged and sounds were abnormal. He became jaundiced on the second day with elevated bilirubin level, which was falling by the sixth day. He died at 10 days, after increasing cardio respiratory difficulty and evidence of infection.

Visible congenital abnormalities included hirsutism, receding forehead, low-set abnormal pinnae, atretic external auditory canals, port-wine stain over distribution of trigeminal nerve, enophthalmos, depressed nasal bridge, short nose, everted nostrils, high arched palate, protruding maxilla, short webbed neck, barrel-shaped chest, short limbs, Simian creases, broad stubby hands and feet, abnormal toes, feet in valgus, absent femoral pulses, small penis and undescended testicles.

Chest x-ray showed abnormal cardiac silhouette. The trachea was narrowed or compressed with a soft tissue swelling over the sternum. Barium swallow showed abnormal mechanism with medium flowing into the nasopharynx and tracheal aspiration which did not produce a cough reflex. The soft palate was poorly developed. The esophagus was displaced to the left. There was slight shortening of the humeri and femora. The digits were short and metacarpals and metatarsals were broad. The radial heads were dislocated.

Autopsy

At autopsy the weight was 3,108 g, crown-rump length 33.6 cm. and the crown-head length 46.5 cm. The following findings were reported.

[1] Central nervous system: flattening of midportion of base of skull with inconspicuous styloid processes, shallow occipital bone, fenestration of flax and laceration in its anterior half and flattening of gyri and narrowing of sulci.

[2] Cardiovascular system: heart enlarged, all chambers distended and walls thickened, high interventricular defect, widely patent ductus arteriosus and pulmonary artery distended.

[3] Abdomen: slight annular constriction of duodenum by pancreas, kidneys 47 g. (normal 23.6 g.), testicles high in abdomen and present in relation to persistent mullerian system, two rudimentary uterine horns posterior to bladder. Adrenal glands together weighed only 5.9 g; microscopically the fetal cortex was still present but degenerating.

Other abnormalities included general vascular congestion, pulmonary edema, hemorrhage, hyalinelike membranes, bacterial bronchopneumonia, sepsis, enteritis, thrombosis of vein of Galen, cerebral edema, and pontine hemorrhages. (W. Bell, personal communications, 1973).

LETTER # 2

The next letter is from Chris and Jena Archer of Marlton, New Jersey.

We recently received some very important medical information that affected us in many ways. Unfortunately, it was too late to spare us from heartache, pain and suffering. We feel that because this is something that is hereditary and runs in the White/LeBlanc family, everyone should be aware of it. We hope that no one else has to go through what we did because of lack of information.

Well to the nitty gritty. A number of us in the family carry an "Inverted 3rd Chromosome." A simple blood test, called a "Karyotype of the blood," can detect if you have this. If you do, then your healthy children should also be tested. If you do not, then based on the research, your child would not be affected.

Why is having this "Inverted 3rd Chromosome" important? If you conceive a child, there is a chance your child could receive either a "short" or a "long" 3rd chromosome. In either case the child will be faced with severe developmental problems. With a "short" 3rd chromosome, typically the embryo is unable to develop. With a "long" 3rd chromosome, the fetus does develop, however, the chromosome has duplicated/deleted portions.

The 3rd chromosome is the third largest chromosome and is an intricate component in the baby's development. It dramatically affects every living cell during development, including the heart, brain, kidneys and bones. The majority of these pregnancies miscarry, usually in the first trimester, but not all do. Unfortunately, those that do not miscarry, may go undetected until birth, unless an amniocentesis/cordocentesis is done during the pregnancy.

A cordocentesis can be done as early as 8-12 weeks into the pregnancy. This is where a sample of blood is drawn from the placenta and then tested for any chromosomal disorders. An amniocentesis can be done around 16 weeks, or later into a pregnancy. This is where a sample of the amniotic fluid is taken and then tested for any chromosomal disorders.

BACK OF THE POND

Being a carrier does not mean that you cannot have healthy children. As you probably know, we have three. Fortunately/unfortunately we found out, through ultrasound in the 21st week of pregnancy with our fourth child, that the baby had severe heart disease. This led us to further testing that unveiled a "long" 3rd chromosome in our baby. It was during this time that we found out about the "Inverted 3rd Chromosome" and that Jena was a carrier. It is difficult to find information on this exact problem, as it is very rare and possibly only found in our ancestry.

Due to political issues in the United States, if you are beyond the 20th week of pregnancy, even if you know that you child will not live, you may not have the choice to go into premature labor, even if it is to preserve the life/health of the mother. This was another issue we had to face.

In summary, if you are a possible carrier of the Inverted 3rd Chromosome and plan on having children, you should have your blood karyotyped. If the test comes back positive, share this information with your doctor immediately. If you conceive a child, you may want to schedule a cordocentesis/amniocentesis early into the pregnancy, to provide you and your doctor with information vital to you and your baby's health. Finding out late in a pregnancy, as we did, can have severe consequences, physically and emotionally.

This letter is written in memory of our son, Daniel Christopher, who was born and died on April 13, 1997.

Chapter 9: Disregard For French and Mi'kmaq Culture

I wish to use the LeBlanc surname when referring to my mother's maiden name. Newfoundland was a British colony before 1949; hence, missionaries, teachers, clergy, inadvertently, or otherwise, changed the name to White, as it would read in English. My mother, like my father, was French in her native tongue. It is interesting to note that in 1899, just two schools existed in the Port au Port-Stephenville district. Both schools housed only French speaking children. At that same time, Mr. John Guy, the teacher at one of those two schools, had indicated that he had much uphill work in teaching the difficult subjects out of English books. I would like to reinstate my mother's identity by reiterating that point. Their mother tongue was taken away by an outside force, not of their own accord; because of circumstances beyond their control, their first language all but died out.

Due to an innate interest in our past, interested parties, like my sister, Melinda, friend Laverne and others, have brought our Mi'kmaq heritage to the forefront. Long after our mother's passing, our family learned that we have Indian status on both sides. Like the French, but even more so, the Mi'kmaq culture was suppressed in my parents' youth. [20] English settlers harbored strong resentment against 'Indians,' and to the majority of people, one Indian was no different from another. My father, born in 1911, speaks highly of his life as a boy. However, it has been highlighted through old census records that few Indians were willing to declare their status. They feared reprisal in the form of ridicule, being treated as outcasts and being subject to abuse while working for non-Indians, etc.

---

[20] Marshall, Ingeborg. *Indian, Beothuk and Micmac: Re-Examining Relationships.* Acadiensis, XVII, 2 (Spring 1988), pp. 52-82. This article can be downloaded from
https://journals.lib.unb.ca/index.php/Acadiensis/article/view/12241/13085

The vote, for example, was another indicator that the Mi'kmaq were once treated differently; mainly as lesser beings. Before 1911, status Indians were not allowed to vote; thus, if you declared your status, you had to be prepared to take the abuse that went with it. Very few were willing to take that chance, because of what their children would have to endure. It appears my father's family fell within that category as well. As my parents had always done with the French language, they also kept our Indian ancestry a secret, for fear we would suffer for it in school.

In wartime, the Indian people were treated differently. There was much confusion in both WWI and WWII as to whether or not Indians should be allowed to serve their country.

BEFORE EUROPEAN SETTLEMENT

Before the Europeans settled in western Newfoundland, the Mi'kmaq lived happy, productive lives. There was plenty of fish to eat, animals to trap and to hunt; small and big game alike such as ermine, fox, rabbit and caribou. They depended on their hunting and fishing to both clothe them and sustain them for food. By the end of the 19th century, the culture and livelihood of the Mi'kmaq people was being threatened by big changes to the landscape of the west coast. Amongst the greatest threats were the completion of the Newfoundland Railway in 1898 and the opening of the Grand Falls paper mill in 1909. The railway cut off important migratory routes of the caribou and newcomers and sportsmen came in large numbers to hunt big and small game. The tree cutting damaged habitats and ecosystems; as a result, the large herd of nearly 300,000 caribou was nearly wiped out. The hunting and trapping that had once sustained the Mi'kmaq was now steadily declining.

Considered poor and illiterate in the eyes of the newcomers, the Mi'kmaq people were looked upon as lazy and uneducated; so, too, were they stigmatized as savages and Jackatars. The term "jackatar" referred to a half-breed, a mixture of French and Mi'kmaq descent; hence, the nickname "jacktar" or "jackatar," as the Benoit's and others were known to have been called.

BACK OF THE POND

According to the Dictionary of Newfoundland English, the Mi'kmaq were looked upon unfavorably in the 1800s, and referred to with terms that were meant to be less than endearing, such as jackatar, jackie tar, jackitar, jack-o-tar, jackotaw and jacky tar with tar referring to the color of their skin.[21] Quoting from this same source, it was written that "Jack-o-tars are a lawless, indolent people, and I am told addicted to thieving. They are looked upon by the English and French as a degraded race, hence styled Jack-o-tars or runaways."[22] The term "runaway" or "outlaw" often referred to the plight of the French fisherman who, for any number of reasons (mistreatment, hunger, tyranny or other social or economic stresses), resorted to jumping ship and deserting, in the hope of finding a better life. It is further shared, in the Dictionary of Newfoundland English, that "in the forties, francophones [in Newfoundland] suffered discrimination and were labeled Jackatars."[23] In one French census of Placentia, Newfoundland, in 1687, the Mi'kmaq were referred to as "savages."[24]

In my opinion though, the Mi'kmaq were far from lazy or uneducated. They had lived productive lives, independent of others, until major changes impacted their natural habitat.

Like their allies, the French, the Mi'kmaq people were Roman Catholic. Since the 1800s, they had assimilated into the culture of the French, and vice versa. They, like the French, were known to have made yearly pilgrimages on July 26 to Cape Breton for the Feast of Saint Anne, their patron saint.

It is probably no coincidence, then, that my mother showed such reverence to St. Anne before her death, considering her Mi'kmaq ancestry. The Mi'kmaq were also documented as having made trips to St. Pierre, where they received religious counseling from French priests, who had travelled to Newfoundland in earlier times.

---

[21] http://www.heritage.nf.ca/dictionary/index.php#2376
[22] http://www.heritage.nf.ca/dictionary/index.php#2377
[23] Ibid.
[24] https://journals.lib.unb.ca/index.php/NFLDS/article/view/141/238

BACK OF THE POND

One of the traditions that was carried forward from the Mi'kmaq culture was the ceremonial pointed hat of the women. This hat, typically fashioned out of natural rine material from the birch trees, was shaped into a cone and worn on the head, which served as protection from the weather and pests such as flies.

Another Birthday Party in our neighbourhood (circa 1961). I can recognize Gaultois', Benoit's and Schumph's. Everyone is wearing Mi'kmaq Party Style Hats. Photo courtesy of Lillian Benoit Retieffe.

Instead of showing respect for the inhabitants of western Newfoundland, mainlanders often looked down on the Indians. They abused their homes and culture, their language, customs and ways. This is similar to what Reverend Michael Brosnan alluded to in his book <u>Pioneer History of St. George's Diocese</u> (see Bibliography under Bay St. George category).

BACK OF THE POND

MY FATHER'S HERITAGE

My father's Indian and French heritage showed through in almost everything he did. His longevity was a telltale indicator of how he spent his life as a child. He died in 2005, at the age of ninety-three.

My father learned how to live off the land in the same way his father and grandfather did; in doing so, his Acadian heritage surfaced. He observed how his father worked the land to plant potatoes, turnip, carrots, cabbage and onions, etc. to feed his large family. He witnessed how the crops were then kept in root cellars to ensure a longer life. I remember our cellar in my father's house. It was in an odd place, I thought. It was under our bathroom floor. I'm sure there might have been a good reason for it having been placed there, as opposed to another spot. Yeah, I wonder if it's still there today. Dad observed and learned how to keep and slaughter animals such as pigs, sheep, cows and hens for precious meat, wool, milk, cream, butter, eggs and more. Foods were so wholesome and nutritious then. I witnessed, myself, how he and Mom often washed, carded and spun wool for blankets, homemade socks, sweaters and mitts.

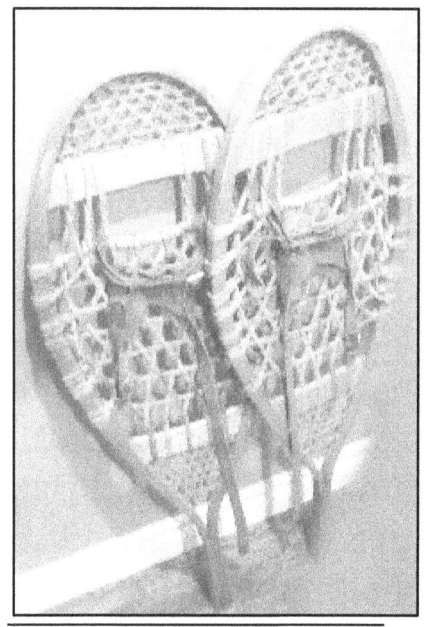

From start to finish, Dad made his own snowshoes; from the cutting of the tree for the bows, the turning of the bows for the snowshoe frame, the slaughtering of the animal for the hide, [25] the curing and tanning of the hide for the laces, to the lacing of the snowshoe, all was done by hand. As a boy, Dad remembered how he wore moccasins, or Mukluks, [26] in the winter months, but went barefoot in the summertime; everybody did, he said.

---

[25] The Cowhide they used to lace the snowshoes they called Babiche, after it had been soaked for a time.
[26] Dad knew how to make Mukluks; if only he still had his tools, he told us.

BACK OF THE POND

Dad told us a story about how Norman Gabriel, also from *Back of the Pond*, showed up at school one day with shoes on. He got a scolding from Monsignor Adams, was told to take off his shoes, and stop showing off. Shoes were not considered a necessity back then.

This reminds me of a story my husband told me about when he was around three or four years old. As the story goes, it was hard to keep shoes on a small child, but still it was thought necessary to keep the child safe, to keep the child free from cutting himself on broken glass or sharp objects. On this day, Bill's mother had to be away for some reason. She got a trusted baby-sitter to care for him and his siblings. It was very hard to keep Bill's shoes on his feet. He kept removing them. After a couple of times having to put his shoes back on, the sitter decided to double-tie the laces. She then gave him a good warning not to remove them again, or if he did, she told him, she was going to hurt his Mom. Bill didn't touch the shoes again; instead, he walked around for the remainder of that day with a nail driven up in his foot. The discovery was made only after his mother returned home that night. I don't think he was overly fond of the sitter, but he clearly proved he dearly loved his Mom.

If my father put his mind to something, he did it. I doubt if he learned that at school, because he left school at the age of 12 and went to the lumber woods to work. I can assure you, I am one of his offspring who has little artistic talent like his. I will admit, though, that I am persistent when I take on a project. My mother, I heard it said often, was very book-smart. She read as much as she could, even medical books, in spite of the fact she had very little schooling. She even diagnosed her brother, Austin's illness as lead poisoning, at a time when there was little known on the subject. Unfortunately, she left us too soon to show her true talents. One of her main goals was to see all her children make it through school. I can remember how good she and Dad were on the old singer sewing machine. Dad would get it into his head to make a tent, one day; another day, a suit of clothes. If I attempted to use the machine, it would keep unthreading and I had little, if any, patience to thread it again.

BACK OF THE POND

Dad was a great fisherman, and he knew how to exaggerate his catch (ha ha). Dad and his nephew, Jimmy Cormier, were very close. They went fishing together often in their late years. On one of those fishing trips, Jimmy lost his false teeth overboard. Sometime later, Dad was out fishing without Jimmy and claimed he caught a large salmon. He told us that when the salmon smiled, he looked just like Jimmy Cormier.

Dad was a sportsman by nature. Whether he was hunting, guiding (in his younger days), picking berries or practicing his shooting, he seemed to have an uncanny knack for everything. He gave whatever he did his undivided attention, just as he did when he told his stories. With tales like *The Golden Arm*, he mesmerized neighborhood children with both his enchantment as well as his charisma. I also remember, after hearing his stories and predictions so many times, how he foresaw that one day we would be able to see the person we were talking to on the telephone. Today we do just that, courtesy of Skype, FaceTime and video chats on Facebook. He was the only one I knew who could sit for hours reading the telephone book; having done so, if he didn't know your name, he could tell you whose family you came from.

Mom, like Dad, also loved the outdoors. I don't remember witnessing this, so it must have been in their early years together. He bragged about how she could outshoot any man. I do remember how we all piled aboard Dad's van to go out blueberry picking; unfortunately, those memories are hazy and few. I mostly remember finding it very warm and not feeling at all well. I remember getting car sick wherever I went, so most trips were not pleasant. I don't remember picking too many berries either. I would be allowed to lie down and rest, while everybody else picked. This brings my thoughts back to a couple of my sick days in school.

I was always involved in the choirs at school. I never, ever, considered choir practice a chore. We sang for masses, Benedictions, and any religious function that allowed us the privilege of singing. The services all took place at the old St. Stephen's church, which had been built in 1909, and burned to the ground on October 19, 1969.

BACK OF THE POND

Roman Catholic Church
Circa: 1962

The Roman Catholic church burned to the ground in the 1960s. A new church now stands in its place.

To get up to the choir, we had to enter the porch, turn left and walk up a set of spiral stairs. The balcony overlooked the congregation below. From the balcony, we, the choir members, lined a set of bleachers, approximately six deep. I recall standing next to Betty-Jean Benoit, who had an angelic voice, singing my heart out, when I started to feel weak. Seconds later, I woke up on the floor below the bleachers. I had passed out and fallen off. Miraculously, I don't remember being hurt. My fainting spells were frequent. Thinking back, it's quite possible that I may have been experiencing low glycemic levels; this would explain why I passed out, after being without food for long periods of time.

The first Friday of every month, we would be marched from the school to the church for mass that began around 11:30 and wasn't over until 12:30 or so. On those days, we fasted after breakfast in the morning, which finished around 8 or 8:15, until mass was over and we had returned home for our dinner at 12:30 or 12:45. I could never make it that long without food. I would get weak and pass out long before mass was over. The fast was an expected and integral part of our religious upbringing. To receive Holy Communion (the symbolic body of Christ), we had to do the fasting and go without food and water for a minimum of three hours.

BACK OF THE POND

The Eucharistic Fast, as it was also called by the clergy, was mitigated by Pope Pius XII, from a complete fast after midnight, to a fast of three hours in 1957; then Pope Paul VI further reduced the requirement for fasting to one hour, in 1964. [27] These changes were intended to encourage Catholics to receive Communion more frequently. The ancient practice was to fast from midnight until mass that day, but as masses in the afternoon and the evenings became common, this was soon modified to fasting for three hours. Current law requires merely one hour of Eucharistic fast, although some Roman Catholics still abide by the older rules.

In our parents' day, and indeed again in our day, we were expected to accept the Catholic Church's set of beliefs, without criticism. I could never deny that this was indoctrination, although I would never have wanted to say that around my mother. It is not surprising that some still abide by the older rules, for any number of personal reasons. The church was always full of people in our younger days. The students were expected to stand up and show respect for their elders. I, however, would always wake up in a seat, after being carried from my lying position on the floor. After the fainting spells, I would always get stomach sick.

I remember well another morning. I'd guess my age to be about ten. Mom had eggs cooked for breakfast, with toast and milk or juice. I loved eggs: fried, boiled or scrambled. But this day, I wasn't feeling well at all, but pretended otherwise, so I could go to music class. My brother, Vernon, a year and a half older than me, was sitting on my right at the kitchen table. We were having a little argument about something minor I'm sure, (can't remember, but wish I could). I was getting the smell of eggs and it was making me nauseous. I nudged Vernon with my elbow. He nudged me back, of course, and without further warning, I fell off my chair, slid under the table and passed out. When I came to, I was being carried to my bedroom; no choir for me, again.

---

[27] Taken from *Catholic Answers: What's the rule for fasting after communion?* located at https://www.catholic.com/qa/whats-the-rule-for-fasting-after-communion

Chapter 10: Lamente de Mon Père

My father often lamented that his freedoms were taken away as he aged. Our world, so different from the past, is a monetary world. We've allowed the trading off of our freedoms, one by one, so we can live in a world that's more technologically advanced. We've reached a point where we are controlled from a distance. Decisions that affect us are no longer left in our hands, but in the hands of those who hold the power, the prestige, the money.

Donald Trump may have it right after all. We seem to have become a world obsessed by celebrities. Even our Prime Minister, Justin Trudeau, is being referred to as Mr. Selfie. We, the world, have lost vision; we are awestruck. We live in the now, often with no, or little, regard for the future. Our children no longer save for a rainy day. That's not totally their fault, I might add. The banks and credit unions are so much to blame, sending cheques and credit cards through the mail at every convenient opportunity. Quick cash vendors are open 24/7, at exorbitant rates. *No credit, bad credit, call us* they entice. We seem to have reached a point where our lawmakers no longer see what is important. Decisions are being made on a global scale. We may well have become collateral damage. Our basic structure appears to be crumbling. Our country's richest resource, its people, is not being utilized properly. For the sake of technology, our resources are being abused.

Looking back to my father's day, it was the little things that made him happy. He had the freedom to go down to the pond by his home, whenever he felt the need or the urge to do so. He could spend hours casting, fishing and wading in the water, to hook one bigger than the last. He could also go down to the pond on short notice, to catch a salmon for his mother to boil up for supper. The fish, he told us, were always utilized. He said, for instance, that he used to drink cups full of cod liver oil from an old fish barrel. Codfish oil had many purposes; prevention of arthritic pain was just one. Drinking of cod oil may be another possible reason my father lived to age 93 *without* arthritis.

My father, Paddy Benoit, with his catch of the day.

Today we can only fish when, where, what and how we are allowed, with permission from an outside source (the long arm of the law again), provided we have the money to buy a license first. Sometimes, get this for good sport, we are only allowed to hook the fish and then release it back into the waters, damaged. Humane? I don't think so. Practicing good conservation? Again, I can't see how. Are these the wise decision makers that we want our children to look up to?

As of this date, there are just a few eel licenses left in the Bay St. George area, and recreational fishing for fresh water eels will soon be discontinued. Dad loved to fish eels; he loved the taste and he considered them a real treat, but today, eels are yet another species of fish that are very limited to fishers, like my father and his offspring. They aren't being discontinued because of their low numbers, by the way; they are rather plentiful in areas such as Flat Bay, here in the Bay St. George area.

BACK OF THE POND

From Flat Bay, eels are caught, boxed and shipped to Nova Scotia to be processed. After processing, they are sold to places like the European Union, where they are considered a delicacy and yield a high market value. Still, did it ever occur to officialdom to explore the ever-increasing market for under-utilized species, such as eels, and to get an inventory of inland waters for such species?

In my father's day, rabbit was hunted for its fur, as well as for food. As boys, Dad said they loved the sportsmanship, the pleasure it gave them and their families to be able to provide food, and yet to be busy doing something they loved. Can you even think of any such sport that children are allowed to do whenever they want, and can do for free? Hunting rabbit was free in my father's youth. Today, to catch rabbit, you have to buy a license. With that license, you are limited by when and how you hunt. Another outside party, from who knows where, determines the method, the type and size of wire, etc. And God forbid you ever have a problem with those rules and regulations. For instance, if you see that, in using government regulated wire (versus your own), your rabbit gets maimed each time and dies a slow dragged-out death, you are *still* obliged to follow those rules, even though you know full well that the results will be detrimental to both you and those animals. My point is that rules and regulations are often made by misguided people who have little, if any, hands-on experience, that would qualify them to make a well-informed and wise ruling. Such decisions are often made from afar, but they would be much better made by the hunter. Such decisions remove our freedom to think for ourselves.

In my father's day, the people were not constantly forbidden access to trails, dirt roads, ponds, rivers and cabins, or charged fees to gain access. Roads, bridges and trails don't just pop up everywhere when we need them. They are built with taxes, that we have paid throughout our lives. We should not have to pay to access those trails a second time, with trail stickers. Once again, decisions are being made for us by a specialized few, decisions that should remain in our hands. Our freedom of movement is sadly jeopardized, but because someone "up-along" does it, we must do it too.

BACK OF THE POND

As stated some time earlier, up until the 1890s, caribou herds roamed Newfoundland in the thousands. Locals, Mi'kmaq and others, relied upon that caribou, mainly as a food supply, but also for every conceivable need they had. Skins, innards, bones, tendons and sinew were all used for clothing, tools, ropes, lines, strings, jewelry, thread, snowshoe laces, mats, blankets, and so on. [28] Nothing was wasted; caribou sustained their lives. But the coming of the railroad to Newfoundland brought many visitors. In turn, the caribou rack became a show of masculinity among the elite. It became a prized possession. Hard times came to those who, for so long, had made their living off the land and all it had to offer. Large piles of caribou carcasses dumped at St. John's harbor were somber proof of the devastation that had taken place at that time.

The Dominion of Newfoundland set out to populate the island with moose, the largest member of the deer family. They did this to entice others to visit our province. The moose were not native to Newfoundland, as were the Woodland Caribou. A first attempt had already been made in 1878, but was unsuccessful. However, in 1904, two bulls and two cows were brought over by train from New Brunswick, Canada. The moose were circled, lassoed by men on snowshoes, tied up and dragged to a waiting sled with high sides. They were then led by horses to the train station, where they made the trip by train to North Sydney.

---

[28] https://en.wikipedia.org/wiki/Mi'kmaq#History

BACK OF THE POND

They crossed on the SS Bruce ferry to Port aux Basques, and travelled by train to central Newfoundland. They were then set free in the woods of Howley, where they prospered. By 1972, there were an estimated 40,000 moose from those meager beginnings.

The first regulated season of moose hunting took place in 1935, with just 80 licenses. From 1945, up until 2005, it is believed that approximately 180,000 moose were legally hunted. As mentioned earlier, the Mi'kmaq did not waste, as newcomers did, the valuable resource they had in big game like caribou or moose. In earlier years, every part of these large animals was put to use for necessities that were not readily available. Even the head was cooked to make pot-head, which I can remember to be delicious and nutritious. Few people cook it today. It was somewhat like pâté or potted meat, very tasty, and was either sliced or used as a sandwich or cracker spread.

My father hunted caribou and moose freely in his younger years. Common sense and word of mouth went a long way in determining whether a bull, a cow, or a calf was taken. Consequently, he learned far more about the herd than we do, since all of our decisions are made for us.

While it may not be a bad idea to put regulations on the moose hunt, why again must we always need to pay for [1] hunting tests, [2] moose licenses year after year, and [3] firearm certificates that have renewal fees?

Not every Newfoundlander can afford to pay for a license. It gets more expensive each year. Licenses on vehicles, trailers, etc. increase household costs, so that it doesn't always pay to hunt. Gas and gas taxes weigh the Newfoundlander down. While this is one sport that should be made more accessible to locals, it is gradually being forfeited to outsiders and trophy hunters. This will ensure a hefty cash flow, at a much higher price tag, for our governing bodies.

BACK OF THE POND

Mercedes Benoit-Penney (another successful moose hunt) Fall 2016

This is what it costs today for the privilege of hunting. Information was taken from 2016 Newfoundland and Labrador Trappers and Hunter's Guide.

MOOSE LICENSE	**CARIBOU LICENSE**
Resident $52.00	Resident $52.00
Senior Resident $33.80	Senior Resident $33.80
Non Resident $502.00	Non-Resident $675.00
BLACK BEAR LICENSE	**SMALL GAME LICENSE ***
Resident Labrador $35.10	Resident small game coyote (combined) $10.00
Senior Labrador $22.80	Resident small game coyote (senior) $6.50
New Resident $39.00	Non Resident small game coyote (Canadian) $50.00
Senior Resident $25.35	Non Resident small game coyote (Alien) $100.00
Non Resident $150.00	Youth (under 16) snaring only FREE

* Small Game license includes Ptarmigan, Grouse, Hare, Coyote

BACK OF THE POND

TRAPPERS LICENSE	GUIDE LICENSE	WOLF SHOOTING LICENSE (Labrador)
General Trapper's License $15.00	Guide License $10.00	Wolf Shooting $25.00
General Trapper's Senior $9.75	Guide License Senior $6.50	Wolf Shooting Senior $16.25
Beaver/Trapline Island $15.00		
Beaver/Trapline Senior $9.75		

It is also important to note that ......

[1] Licenses sold through vendor outlets and/or government service centers are subject to an additional $3 fee at the time of purchase.

[2] All licenses are non-refundable and subject to change.

[3] Prices shown do not yet show HST.

[4] License fees for seniors apply to those 65 and older.

CANADIAN MIGRATORY GAME BIRD HUNTING PERMIT
Ducks, Murres, Geese and Snipe
Resident $17.00
Non Resident (Canadian) $17.00
Non Resident (Alien) $17.00

Just last week, I heard rumblings on a radio talk show about the possibility of adding yet another license to our sport fishery; this time, a license to fish trout. As another old saying goes, if Dad hears this, he must be turning in his grave by now. I asked earlier if you could recall any sport from the past that still remained free. Some of you may have thought of trouting; well, it seems someone is one step ahead of you. If you, your children or your grandchildren, have been enjoying a free day of trout fishing at your favorite pond, beware; someone, possibly from the upper class, sees dollar signs that can be made at your expense. Our government will never have enough money. They think globally, like the banks. The fact that the conversation has already taken place shows just how far removed we are from the freedoms of our parents and grandparents. The rich resources, in Newfoundland and Labrador, should remain here for us to reap benefits from, and to be left as a legacy for our children and grandchildren. Yet our governments have such short-sighted vision for anything other than the almighty dollar.

In my dad's day, he could cut wood for the winter's heat. He could get his wood when, where and how he saw fit; because the choices were his, it was his responsibility to make sure he didn't cut on private property, or do damage to the lakes and rivers, etc. He told us that people grew up with respect for one another. They all helped where they could, and if they owed their neighbor, they always tried to pay back in full. Money, however, was not always needed. People could barter or return favors to keep in each other's good graces. There was a feeling of pride at the end of the day, a feeling of accomplishment, a day well lived. Today, you can still burn wood for your winter's heat. However, to do so, you must buy a license each year. That license will dictate when, where, how and how much you are allowed to cut. Again, regulating some of these terms may not be a bad idea, especially where large numbers of people cut, but why must the emphasis always be on money?

Newfoundland is forever changing. That's the way our decision makers seem to want it. Our rural areas, stripped of services, have to rely on the cities for health services, dumping sites, schools and more. We are all taxed with the commitment that we get equal health benefits, yet, it looks suspiciously unfair that one would have to be on a waiting list for three years, seven months and twenty-six days, in order to get a hearing test done in Stephenville. Yet this is exactly how long it took for my requisition. We have only one person hired in this position to serve our area of the west coast. In fact, I am surprised we can access an audiology department here at all.

Services are increasingly moving to the larger center of Corner Brook, some one hundred kilometers away from my home town in Port au Port West. Our local airport has been stripped of its viability and in the past year CFSX radio station in Stephenville was removed by Steele Communications.

> **Western Health**
> **AUDIOLOGY**
>
> P.O. Box 2005
> Corner Brook, NL A2H 6J7
> Phone: (709) 637-5374
> Fax: (709) 637-5381
>
> 127 Montana Drive
> Rehab Annex
> Stephenville, NL A2N 2T4
> Phone: (709) 643-8690
> Fax: (709) 643-3944
>
> Date: *February 10, 17*
> Re: *Mercedus Penney*
> DOB: *June 6, 1951*
>
> *MArch 8 Wed. 10:00*
>
> Dear *Mercedus*,
>
> A request for you / your child to have a hearing assessment at the Audiology Department was received on *July 8, 2013*.
>
> If you are still interested in this service, please call our department at 643-8690 between 8:30 a.m. – 4:30 p.m. to arrange an appointment. If we do not hear from you by *March 3, 2017*, your name will be removed from our waitlist, and a new referral will be required for future service.
>
> Thank you,
>
> *Sharon Grandy, Steno II*
> Audiology Department
>
> **WESTERN HEALTH IS SCENT-FREE. PLEASE NO PERFUMES, COLOGNES, HAIRSPRAYS, ETC. THOSE WEARING SCENTED PRODUCTS WILL BE ASKED TO RESCHEDULE APPOINTMENTS.**

Another startling fact is that, with our baby-boomer population of mostly seniors, we have to travel to Corner Brook to see an Ophthalmologist. This fact is appalling, especially in the winter months. Each trip is a full day, requires a driver, and takes anywhere from two to five hours of waiting in the doctor's office.

To add to the inconvenience, we are now required to make the trip twice in one week; one day to get the required testing, another day to speak to the doctor. Many seniors, like my husband and I, have glaucoma, which requires three or four visits a year. These trips are a huge burden, both financially and otherwise. This is not equal treatment by Western Health.

There appears to be a major push to be more like other provinces, yet numerous people who live in other provinces, are not even allowed to put up a clothesline. So much for attracting tourists to Newfoundland with videos of colored homemade quilts flapping on the line in the fresh smog-less air, if we are always to mimic another province's footsteps. We have our own unique, pristine province. We can benefit more by making our own decisions.

We, the taxpayers, are being taken advantage of, every time greedy government wants another dollar. They've removed our freedoms. Now, we are barely recognizable. Some like to call that progress, but I think we've already paid too big a price for that so-called progress. As I've said before, some have lost sight of what is most important, our most prized possession, our people.

"You only know what it's all about when you're ready to die," my father told us, when he reached his elder years. When he no longer had the capacity to hunt, to fish, to visit his friends, or to walk, then he had so much time to reflect on his life, and to see what really mattered. He didn't have a lot of regrets, but he did have some, and they weren't that he didn't save more money. In fact, they had nothing to do with money. They were about not helping others enough.

Do you remember ever being told as a child that you should learn from your elders? You were told that, because the oldest people in your communities had lived and could give indispensable advice. Yet most of the current generation cannot fathom the idea of saving for a rainy day, preparing for the future, or helping their neighbors.

BACK OF THE POND

Our elders have a wisdom that cannot be bought, that can only be acquired through experience; maybe that is why it is so difficult to give advice to the young, advice that they will heed. Until they experience it for themselves, they cannot fully understand; if this is so, we are all destined to falter.

In truth, if we are to experience in order to understand, we have to be shown the way. Who better to show us that way than our elders? The Indian ways of the past were carried out with such patience. They were not interrupted constantly by bells and whistles, beeps and deadlines. Multi-tasking wasn't in the vocabulary. Children had only to observe their elders and strive to please them. Today, we're too far removed from what makes a person happy. Children don't seem to find fulfillment in playing computer games, drinking, smoking, doing drugs or partying. They appear lost in most everything they do. They are bored with life as it is. They need change. I suggest they *look back* to find their way.

Chapter 11: Paradise Lost

During World War II, in 1941, the United States of America set up army, air and naval bases in Newfoundland. Bases were set up in Stephenville, Argentia and St. John's, to name just three.

Aerial view of Ernest Harmon Air Force Base runways
Stephenville, Newfoundland circa 1942
John Cardoulis Photograph Collection

In each case, the land they chose for their base was already inhabited by homeowners and landowners. These property owners had to be bought out and relocated to accommodate the American occupation, which was so vital to the war effort. As claims moved forward, there was much controversy as to the dollar value of properties on the east coast versus the west coast of the island.

BACK OF THE POND

St. John's, being the capital city of Newfoundland, housed the more affluent English-speaking dignitaries and merchants, as opposed to the mostly unschooled Acadian people. Yet, that was little reason to pay less to the property owners on the west coast, for land that was equally or more valuable, especially during wartime.

On the contrary, unlike those who lived in St. John's, the French Acadian people who populated the Indian Head or *Back of the Pond* area of land at the time were self-sufficient. The Acadians depended totally on the land and sea for sustenance. They maintained their livelihood by utilizing local natural resources to the fullest. They cultivated their land for growing root crops and their pastureland was used for their animals, such as cows, sheep, fowl and horses. Horses were used for hauling, as well as for transportation; cows were used for dairy products and sheep served them well for wool products and for food. The Bay was teeming with cod, halibut, herring, salmon and lobster, as well as other shellfish. Herring was a natural fertilizer for the cultivated fields and cod-liver oil was an all-purpose remedy and lubricant. They even shipped fresh salmon to Nova Scotia via rail and ferry. Seals were more specific to certain seasons of the year. Fruit trees were planted; berries were grown and wild berries were picked. The local forests provided firewood for heating, and logs for sawmills. Some trees were used for medicinal purposes (i.e. spruce gum for healing, juniper bark and juniper berries for health purposes, such as poultices, etc.).

In winter, the people trapped for animals, furs and food. They were able to obtain cash by selling these furs, as well as selling their fresh salmon. Their root crops could keep well in cellars all year round. In late spring, ice blocks that had been sawn from a nearby pond, would be hauled on hand sleds, placed in a sawdust enclosure and utilized when needed to ship salmon. Some liviers, whose homes were more exposed to the elements, moved inland to winter houses, where there was more shelter from the winds and the cold during the winter months.

Generally, recreation *Back of the Pond* consisted of fly fishing and trouting, swimming, horse-racing (on and off the ice), snowshoeing, skating and sledding, just to name a few activities.

BACK OF THE POND

The following pictures, courtesy of the Stephenville Historical Society Museum, are of a United States military unit that came to the Stephenville area to set up a base for the war efforts in the year 1941. This unit was made up of different building trades, surveyors and engineers. This battalion could do any jobs and complete any tasks assigned, such as docks, runways, roads, etc. These were the military personnel responsible for changing the face of *Back of the Pond*. Their commander was Lieutenant Colonel Wayne G. West. The picture that follows shows a sizeable part of the U.S. Army construction battalion with troop living quarters (tents), and part of a root crop field in the background, and to the right.

Courtesy of Stephenville Historical Society Museum

Once the Americans had expropriated the area, much of it cultivated, they decided to use some of the land to provide root vegetables and corn for the mess halls, to feed their troops. Mr. James Jollimore was hired by the Americans to oversee the project. The farms on *Back of the Pond* and the ocean side of Stephenville Pond were used for this purpose. Much of the cultivated land is situated where Harmon Seaside Links Golf Course is today. There is still evidence of where these farms were, in the form of wild peas, apples and gooseberries.

The Americans ceased operation of their farms in 1955. Bunkers still exist in the golf course area. As well, some bunkers were used for ammunition storage, while others were used as root crop cellars. One of those bunkers is visible on Massachusetts Drive, on the way to Little Port Harmon.

Despite the position that people of the Stephenville area were in, government administrators in St. John's worked *against* equal treatment. Along with the expropriation of the land, predominantly Acadian families had to be relocated. This, in itself, was a very trying and traumatic experience. They didn't know what was going to happen to their animals, where they were to relocate, or whether they would find fertile acreage. Most of the cultivated land had already been utilized in the surrounding district. The loss was immeasurable, and now, the Acadians had to face an establishment that showed little sympathy to their plight.

BACK OF THE POND

Instead of treating all parties fairly, an agreement was made to pay out the following dollar amounts.

St. John's, Quidi Vidi — $400 per acre

Argentia — $300 per acre

Stephenville — $250 per acre

In addition to higher values for their land, property owners in St. John's and Argentia also received an extra 20 percent added onto the claim amount for disturbance, as they called it. Stephenville, by comparison, yet again, only received 10 percent.

I think it is definitely worth mentioning that the government justified this double standard by arguing that Stephenville residents did not experience as much disturbance as the residents of St. John's.

Of the three communities cited here, there is no doubt in my mind that Stephenville had the most to lose. Many families, perhaps all, would have preferred to remain where they were. Some argued that their livelihood was dependent on that land. They worked the land and provided themselves and their children with all the necessities; they led happy, productive lives, independent of dole or handouts from the government. They were reluctant to leave, for fear they would no longer be able to support their large families.

The land the residents lived on before the expropriation was rich, arable land: completely agreeable to cultivating, to raising crops, to feeding, breeding and raising livestock and to plowing and tilling, as was needed. This was difficult, if not impossible, to find in close proximity. The liviers, of course, wanted to resettle nearby, to be close to their families and friends. Some families resettled along Blanche Brook, for example, or on West Street or Kippens; other families moved into the outskirts of Stephenville and beyond, to settle in other communities on the west coast. However, they would never be as well off as they were before.

BACK OF THE POND

The dollar amounts paid out in claims varied with the individual owners and their attitude towards the negotiators. Some settled immediately for the smaller amounts, to avoid the stress of the dragged-out process that lay ahead. Others settled without complaint or deliberation; they considered the act of moving a service to their country (a small price to pay towards the war effort). Still others refused to sell for the little they were offered, and held out for more; closer to replacement value. Some families had relocated and not received their money for many months, placing them in dire positions, unable to pay rent or feed their own families.

A number of factors appear to have worked against the people of Stephenville. Since they were situated so far away from the capital, government administrators, store owners and merchants were unaware of the resourcefulness of the Acadian dwellers. They were indifferent to the hardships of the outport people, and considered them deserving of a lesser amount. They failed to consider that without their cultivated land, many might be forced into poverty. It is interesting to note that the Americans were more sympathetic to the plight of the displaced people.

The Americans immediately recognized the importance of Stephenville. They chose it because it was an ideal setting for the military and its war efforts. It was in a strategic location, on major airline routes from North America to Europe. It was also an excellent location for shipping, being closer to the north-eastern seaboard of the U.S.A., as well as central Canada. This made it perfect for access to those industrial areas. Also, the Bay St. George area was much closer to Newfoundland's gulf ferry link to the Maritimes. It defies reason why the St. John's establishment was so unwilling to accept those realities as readily as our American friends.

Language didn't appear to be a barrier to them. A little bit of diplomacy goes a long way. In one case, the Base provided milk to displaced families for at least a year. Individual acts of charity by the Americans were not unusual. There was another case of an American civilian noticing a hungry child, and reporting it to the American military. The commander, in turn, ensured that the family was provided for.

BACK OF THE POND

Another reason for the disparity was that the English-speaking dignitaries thought that the French-speaking Acadians were uneducated because they could not speak the English language. They were so biased in their views that they failed to see the irony in the fact that they, themselves, didn't speak French.

The following is yet another example of the debasing of the French language.

Of the two official church documents that follow, both are made out for the same person; however, the latest document, dated 1904, had all French names changed to English, even those of the witnesses. As well, the officiating priest was English, unlike the first certificate from 1878.

CERTIFICATE OF BAPTISM

St. Stephen's Parish
Stephenville, Newfoundland

Canada   A2N 1E4

Name: Thomas LeBlanc

Father: Damas LeBlanc

Mother's Maiden Name: Mary Royer

Born on March 9, 1878 at Stephenville

BAPTISED on April 22, 1878

ACCORDING TO THE RITE OF THE ROMAN CATHOLIC CHURCH

by Rev. Joseph Vierenneau

Sponsors: Clement Bourgeois

Esther Royer

Confirmed on

Marginal Notations:

Date: May 27, 2003

Priest: *Maurice O'Quinn*

CERTIFICATE OF MARRIAGE

St. Stephen's Parish
Stephenville, Newfoundland
Canada   A2N 1E4

Thomas White   and   Julianna White

were lawfully married on   August 18, 1904

ACCORDING TO THE RITE OF THE ROMAN CATHOLIC CHURCH
AND IN CONFORMITY WITH LAWS OF THE PROVINCE OF NEWFOUNDLAND

Father of the Groom: Damase White   Mother of the Groom: Mary Royer
Father of the Bride: Anthony White   Mother of the Bride: Julianna Hynes

Officiating Minster: P. W. Brown
In the presence of: Charles White
and Julia White

As appears from the Marriage Register of this Parish.

Licence No.

Date: June 02, 2004

Priest   *Maurice O'Quinn*

BACK OF THE POND

Undoubtedly, the merchant community in St. John's was able to influence the Commission Government at the time. Whatever the reason, liviers from *Back of the Pond* or Indian Head or Acadian Village, as it was referred to before it was officially named Stephenville, were done an injustice.

It took Commission of Government in St. John's approximately five years to complete all land claims.

In the land claims report, there was a brief mention of several islands that confirms my father's story of four islands laid claim to in an earlier chapter. This brief statement can be found on page 89 of "From Outport to Base: The American Occupation of Stephenville, 1940-1945" by Steven High. [29]

Before listing homes and landowners from that time, I wish to reiterate the existence of several small islands that were once in Stephenville Pond, near the Golf Course Club House. Please keep in mind that when the channel to the pond was constructed, the elevation of the pond changed, when it was opened up to the sea, causing the water to recede and the islands to disappear.

Please note that, once again, many names were changed from French to English. This was another thoughtless gesture and bold injustice done to the French Acadian people.

---

[29] https://spectrum.library.concordia.ca/976909/1/stephenville_article.pdf

BACK OF THE POND

The following is a list of homes and landowners from the expropriation days (1938-1952) as per the Department of Public Works, Newfoundland Board of Arbitration Record Photographs. [30]

This sub-series consists of 265 photographs (black and white) relating to 145 record claims for remuneration for expropriated property in the community of Stephenville.

The images illustrate houses, fences, shops, sheds, farms, farm animals, vehicles, buildings, and household items.

Also included are the claim numbers as well as a brief description of the properties that were bought out when the American Base came to the Stephenville area.

Many of the house-holders have similar last names as extended families were often uprooted as a result of expropriation. Original claim numbers have been retained.

If you were to conduct a title search for Stephenville Claims for Compensation, you can further access 5 records that denote the claimant names alphabetically. It needs to be shared that there were far more claims for compensation than there are photographs; however, all records containing photographs are indicated by an asterisk (*).

As denoted on page 93 of "From Outport to Base: The American Occupation of Stephenville, 1940-1945" by Steven High [31] ...... The Stephenville Claims came in three waves during the war. The first batch of 12 claims (1S to 12S) were resolved by December 1941. After the base expanded, the Board of Compensation travelled to Stephenville in July 1942 to hear another 41 cases (13S to 56S) and returned again in July 1943 to consider yet another 128 claims (57S to 185S).

---

[30] http://gencat.eloquent-systems.com/therooms_permalink.html?key=38234
[31] https://spectrum.library.concordia.ca/976909/1/stephenville_article.pdf

BACK OF THE POND

Property of Patrick Bennett, Stephenville
Father of Author
(A 65-26)
1943-1944
Claim # 110S

BACK OF THE POND

Property of Austin and Rodney White, Stephenville
Maternal Uncles of Author
(sons of Tom LeBlanc and Julianna LeBlanc)
(A 66-50, A 66-51, A 66-52, A 66-53, A 66-54, A 66-55, A 66-56, A 66-57)
1943-1944
Claim # 128S

Eight views: large barn; shed at back of barn; sawmill; wood-lot; house with cow lying in front; shed behind house; small sheds and sawhorse; and fenced hay field.

BACK OF THE POND

Property of James Bennett, Stephenville
Paternal Grandfather of Author
(A 65-10, A 65-11, A 65-12)
1944-1945
Claim # 79S

Three views: House and barn; barn and henhouse.

BACK OF THE POND

Property of Paul Bennett, Stephenville
(A 65-27, A 65-28, A 65-29)
1943-1944
Claim # 84S

Three views of partially constructed houses.

BACK OF THE POND

Property of Josephine Bennett, Stephenville
(A 65-18, A 65-19, A 65-20)
1941-1944
Claim # 57S

Three views: house; barn; and tar paper covered house.

BACK OF THE POND

Property of Estate of Luke Bennett, Stephenville
(A 65-21, A 65-22, A 65-23, A 65-24)
1943-1944
Claim # 38S
Claim #77S

Four views: barn; fenced farm field; farm shed in fenced field; and farm shed in fenced field.

BACK OF THE POND

Property of Joseph Bennett, Stephenville
(A 65-17)
1943-1945
Claim # 82S

BACK OF THE POND

Property of Adolph Alexander, Stephenville
(A 64-141)
194-
No claim number cited

BACK OF THE POND

Property of Brendon Alexander, Stephenville
(A 64-142)
1943-1944
Claim # 173S

Property of Joseph A. Alexander, Stephenville
(A 64-143, A 64-144)
1943-1944
Claim # 74S

Two views: house with barn and shed; blacksmith shop and shed with firewood and sawhorses.

BACK OF THE POND

Property of Adolph Aucoin, Stephenville
(A 64-145)
1941-1947
Claim # 222S

BACK OF THE POND

Property of William Barry, Stephenville
(A 64-146, A 64-147, A 64-148, A 64-149, A 64-150, A 65-1, A 65-2, A 65-3)
1942-1943
Claim # 16S

Eight views: large two-storied house; two-storied house with additions, front view; two-storied house with additions, back view; barn with wagon; barn with woodpile and clothesline; barn with weather vane; house with additions and woodpile; and large barn.

BACK OF THE POND

Property of Estate of John B. Bennett, Stephenville
(A 65-13, A 65-14, A 65-15, A 65-16)
1941-1944
Claim # 9S

Three views: house with barn and outbuildings; barns and farm sheds; and barn in fenced field.

BACK OF THE POND

Property of Estate of Arsene V. Gallant, Stephenville
(A 65-104)
1940-1945
Claim #11S

BACK OF THE POND

Property of Estate of Arsene V. Gallant, Stephenville
(A 65-105, A 5-106, A 65-107, A 65-108)
(A 65-109, A 65-110, A 65-111, A 65-112)
1943-47
Claim # 87S

Eight views: two haystacks in field; side view of barn; front view of barn; field; one-storied store; one-storied store; large house; warehouse.

Property of Harold Gaudon, Stephenville
(A 65-113)
1943-1949
Claim # 119S

Tar paper house.

BACK OF THE POND

Property of Medrick Gaudon, Stephenville
(A 65-114, A 65-115, A 65-116)
1943-1945
Claim # 118S

Three views: two-storied house with fenced garden; garage with ramp and platform for car repairs; and log construction building.

BACK OF THE POND

Property of Patrick Gaudon, Stephenville
(A 65-117, A 65-118, A 65-119)
1943-1946
Claim # 151S

Three views: large house with sheep outside fenced garden; three small sheds inside fenced field; and large barn with cow in front.

BACK OF THE POND

Property of William Gaudon and John O'Neill, Stephenville
(A 65-120, A 65-121, A 65-122)
1946-1947
Claim # 204S

Three views: large shed near road along ocean; large building in field; and four small buildings in fenced field.

BACK OF THE POND

Property of Francis Anthony Gaultois, George and Michael and Richard J. McIsaac, Stephenville
(A 65-123)
1942
Claim # 18S

View of Gaultois Brothers store.

BACK OF THE POND

Property of Gaultois Bros. and Richard McIsaac, Stephenville
(A 65-124, A 65-125, A 65-126, A 65-127, A 65-128, A 65-129, A 65-130)
1941-1944
Claim # 80S

Seven views: end view of tenement building with wind charger (generator) visible; Gaultois Bros. store with car parked in front; fenced area with three unit tenement house and building used as ice house; large building with storefront; tenement building with six units; back view of large building; front view of large building.

BACK OF THE POND

Property of Harry N. Hallett, Stephenville
(A 65-131)
1942-1944
Claim #94S

Small house with fenced garden.

BACK OF THE POND

Property of Gerald Haynes, Stephenville
(A 65-132)
1941-1942
Claim #6S

Two hay barns on cobble-stone beach.

BACK OF THE POND

Property of Charles H. Hong, Stephenville
(A 65-133)
1941-1942
Claim # 93S

Tar-paper house with wash tub and steel barrels in front.

BACK OF THE POND

Property of Mercier House, Stephenville
(A 65-134)
1943-1944
Claim # 75S

BACK OF THE POND

Property of Mack Hulan, Stephenville
(A 65-135)
1941-1942
Claim # 13S

Two small tar-paper dwellings.

BACK OF THE POND

Property of John Joy, Stephenville
(A 65-136, A 65-137)
1943-1949
Claim # 90S

Two views: large commercial style building; and small garage.

BACK OF THE POND

Property of Martin LaFitte, Stephenville
(A 65-138)
1941-1942
Claim # 15S

Two one-storied buildings. Claim refers to small building on left used as a barber shop.

BACK OF THE POND

Property of Martin LaFitte, Stephenville
(A 65-139)
1942-1946
Claim # 115S

La Fittes Barber Shop.

BACK OF THE POND

Property of Albert March, Stephenville
(A 65-140)
1941-1942
No claim number cited

House with fenced garden and barn.

BACK OF THE POND

Property of Louis March and Gerald A. March, Stephenville
(A 65-141, A 65-142, A 65-143, A 65-144)
1941
No claim number cited

Four views: two-storied house; barn; wood shed; and school building. Image A 65-144 refers to a building on March's property owned by the Roman Catholic Episcopal Corporation.

BACK OF THE POND

Property of Michael March, Stephenville
(A 65-145, A 65-146)
1941
No claim number cited

Two views: two-storied barn with single-storied side additions; and house with outbuildings.

BACK OF THE POND

Property of Stanley March, Stephenville
(A 65-147)
1941-1944
Claim # 39S

View of barn, animal house and shed.

BACK OF THE POND

Property of Stanley March, Stephenville
(A 65-148)
1943-1944
Claim # 117S

House and shed behind fence.

BACK OF THE POND

Property of Susan March, Stephenville
(A 65-149, A 65-150)
1943-1952
Claim # 152S

Two views: house and fence in trees; and small tar-paper building.

BACK OF THE POND

Property of Onzuan Bennett, Stephenville
(A 65-25)
1941
No claim number cited

Partially constructed house.

BACK OF THE POND

Property of William Bennett, Stephenville
(A 65-30, A 65-31)
1941-1948
Claim # 241S

Two images: large shed; and small shed.

BACK OF THE POND

Property of Harvey Bishop and John L. Coleman, Stephenville
(A 65-32, A 65-33, A 65-34)
1942
Claim # 19S

Three views of two commercial buildings used as a bowling alley.

BACK OF THE POND

Property of George Boulos, Stephenville
(A 65-35, A 65-36, A 65-37)
1943-1944
Claim # 88S

Three views: tenement house with 10 living units; Caines cafe (restaurant); tar-papered building.

BACK OF THE POND

Property of George and Paul Boulos, Stephenville
(A 65-38, A 65-39, A 65-40)
1942
Claim # 29S

Three views of two small stores.

Property of George Basha, Stephenville
(A 65-4)
1943
Claim # 69S

Building used as a store and dance hall.

BACK OF THE POND

Property of Paul Boulos, Stephenville
(A 65-41, A 65-42)
1943
Claim # 92S

Two views of row tenement houses. Clothesline hung at end of building.

BACK OF THE POND

Property of Boulos and Company (George and Paul Boulos), Stephenville
(A 65-43, A 65-44, A 65-45, A 65-46, A 65-47)
1946
Claim # 89S

Five views: small drygoods store; barber shop; clothing store with sale signs; row tenement houses; and theatre.

BACK OF THE POND

Property of James Burgois, Stephenville
(A 65-48)
1944
Claim # 171S

BACK OF THE POND

Property of Basil Cormier, Stephenville
(A 65-49, A 65-50)
1943-1948
Claim # 83S

Two views of small house with fence and wind charger (electricity generator).

BACK OF THE POND

Property of John Basha, Stephenville
(A 65-5)
1943-1944
Claim # 101S

BACK OF THE POND

Property of the Estate of Charles Cormier, Stephenville
(A 65-51)
1941-1944
Claim # 33S

Two-storied house with wind charger (electricity generator) and outbuildings.

BACK OF THE POND

Property of Euzeb Cormier, Stephenville
(A 65-52, A 65-53, A 65-54, A 65-55)
1942-1944
Claim # 44S

Four views including: large house with barn, well and pump; small house with clothesline hung with laundry; large barn; and four small outbuildings with wood pile and wooden sled.

BACK OF THE POND

Property of Frank Cormier, Stephenville
(A 65-56)
1943-1945
Claim # 141S

House with cow and cat in front and clothesline at the side.

BACK OF THE POND

Property of Henry Cormier, Stephenville
(A 65-57)
1943-1944
Claim # 178S

House with recently cleared land in foreground.

BACK OF THE POND

Property of Hubert Cormier, Stephenville
(A 65-58)
1943-1944
Claim # 158S

Property of Patrick Cormier, Stephenville
(A 65-59; A 65-60)
1943-1944
Claim # 135S

Two views: house with wood shed and wood pile; large barn with sheep visible in fenced field.

BACK OF THE POND

Property of Margaret Boulos Basha, Stephenville
(A 65-6)
1943
Claim # 70S

Margaret Boulos' retail store.

BACK OF THE POND

Property of Thomas Cormier, Stephenville
(A 65-61)
1943
Claim # 134S

House with large barn and other outbuildings. Also a wind-generator built near side of house.

Property of William Cormier, Stephenville
(A 65-62)
1943-1944
Claim # 142S

House with outbuildings, car parked near house. Child with wagon and chicken in foreground; also, a wind-generator near side of house.

BACK OF THE POND

Property of Estate of Joseph Doucett, Stephenville (A 65-63)
1943-1945
Claim #78S

House with car parked inside front fence.

BACK OF THE POND

Property of Justin Downey, Stephenville
(A 65-64, A 65-65, A 65-66, A 65-67, A 65-68)
1941-1947
No claim number cited

Five views: house; small shed; two barns; large barn; and barn.

BACK OF THE POND

Property of Louis Eddy, Stephenville
(A 65-69; A 65-70)
1942-1944
Claim # 125S

Two views: small shed with fenced yard; and house with wind charger electricity generator mounted on roof.

BACK OF THE POND

Property of Frederick Bennett and Estate of John B. Bennett, Stephenville
(A 65-7, A 65-8)
1943-1944
Claim # 166S

Two views: 1. View of house without buildings [Annotations on photograph]: Farm, hen house, store, woodshed; 2. View of large shed and fenced field.

BACK OF THE POND

Property of Walter Ehrnreiter, Stephenville
(A 65-71)
1942
Claim # 26S

Tar paper cabin with outhouse.

BACK OF THE POND

Property of Augustus Feder, Stephenville
(A 65-72)
1942-1944
Claim # 27S

Building with sign: Gus Feder's Clothing Store.

BACK OF THE POND

Property of Bernard Gabriel, Stephenville
(A 65-73; A 65-74; A 65-75; A 65-76)
1943
Claim # 138S

Four views: tar paper building with partially completed larger building; small house with wind-generator; small building among trees; and small garage.

BACK OF THE POND

Property of Clement Gabriel, Stephenville
(A 65-77; A 65-78; A 65-79)
1943-1949
Claim # 144S

Three views: log building with longer fence in foreground; two storied house with sheds in back; barn with attached fences.

BACK OF THE POND

Property of Gordon Gabriel, Stephenville
(A 65-80)
1943-1944
Claim # 140S

BACK OF THE POND

Property of John Gabriel, Stephenville
(A 65-81)
1941-1948
Claim # 41S

Old barn with hay pile and hay rack.

BACK OF THE POND

Property of John Gabriel, Stephenville
(A 65-82; A 65-83)
1943-1948
Claim # 136S

Two views: large house with Pontiac Woodie station wagon parked in side yard and wind-generator mounted on roof. Small two-door garage next to house; and large barn.

BACK OF THE POND

Property of Julia Gabriel, Stephenville
(A 65-84)
1941-1942
Claim # 51S

House in fenced field.

BACK OF THE POND

Property of Lawrence Gabriel, Stephenville
(A 65-85)
1944-1946
Claim # 132S

Storehouse with well.

BACK OF THE POND

Property of Estate of Margaret Gabriel, Stephenville
(A 65-86; A 65-87; A 65-88; A 65-89; A 65-90)
1941-1943
No claim number cited

Five views: large two-storied house with barn; barn and out-buildings; two barns; two barns; house with clothesline.

BACK OF THE POND

Property of Gerald Bennett, Stephenville
(A 65-9)
1943-1948
Claim # 147S

BACK OF THE POND

Property of Estate of Philip Gabriel, Stephenville
(A 65-91)
1941-1942
No claim number cited

Property of Prime Gabriel, Stephenville
(A 65-92; A 65-93)
1943
Claim # 43S

Two views: small house with shed; and small tar paper building with barn.

BACK OF THE POND

Property of Prime Gabriel, Stephenville
(A 65-94; A 65-95)
1943-1944
Claim # 179S

Two views: house with Pontiac Woodie station wagon in foreground; and group of men next to a log cutter.

BACK OF THE POND

Property of Reginald Gabriel, Stephenville
(A 65-96)
1943-1944
Claim # 139S

House with fence.

BACK OF THE POND

Property of William Charles Gabriel, Stephenville
(A 65-97)
1943-1946
Claim # 159S

Garage with car.

BACK OF THE POND

Property of Estate of Andrew E. Gallant, Stephenville
(A 65-98; A 65-99; A 65-100; A 65-101; A 61-102; A 65-103)
1941-1942
Claim # 1S

Six views: house with fenced garden; cabin; large barn front view; large barn back view; back view of two storage sheds; storage shed.

BACK OF THE POND

Property of William March, Stephenville
(A 66-1)
1940-1941
No claim number cited

Barn and sheds in fenced field.

BACK OF THE POND

Property of James O'Regan, Stephenville
(A 66-10)
1943-1944
Claim # 175S

House with fences.

BACK OF THE POND

Property of Ambrose Payne, Stephenville
(A 66-11)
1943-1945
Claim # 67S

Building used as dwelling and commercial property, including pool room.

BACK OF THE POND

Property of Alan Rideout, Stephenville
(A 66-12)
1943-1944
Claim # 81S

BACK OF THE POND

Property of Ronald Robinson, Stephenville
(A 66-13)
1943-1944
Claim # 155S

BACK OF THE POND

Property of Roman Catholic Episcopal Corporation, St. George's
(A 66-14)
1941-1942
Claim # 12S

Side view of building.

BACK OF THE POND

Property of Roman Catholic Episcopal Corporation, St. George's
Pond School
(A 66-15)
1941-1942
Claim # 121S

BACK OF THE POND

Property of Harold Russell, Stephenville
(A 66-16)
1941
No claim number cited

Property of Joseph F. Russell, Stephenville
(A 66-19, A 66-20)
1943-1944
Claim # 59S

Two views: front view of cottage style house with fenced garden and saltbox style barns; and side view of house with saltbox style barns.

BACK OF THE POND

Property of Harold J. Russell, Stephenville
(A 66-17; A 66-18)
1942-1943
Claim # 127S

Two views: house with wind charger (generator) and well house; and view of well house and shed.

BACK OF THE POND

Property of Telesphore White, Stephenville
(A 66-100)
1943-1944
Claim # 123S

Two large log construction barns.

Property of Vincent White, Stephenville
(A 66-101, A 66-102)
1943-1944
Claim # 106S

Two views: house and shed, women, girl and men near house; and close view of shed.

BACK OF THE POND

Property of William A. White, Stephenville
(A 66-103)
1943-1944
Claim # 76S

BACK OF THE POND

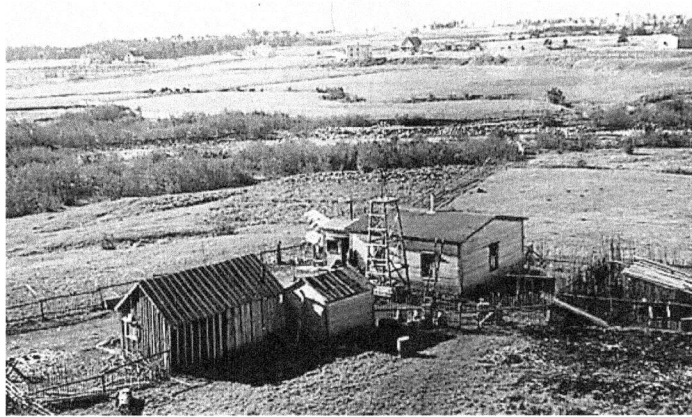

Property of William Henry White, Stephenville
(A 66-104, A 66-105, A 66-106)
1943-1944
Claim # 103S

Three views: small house with shed and [doghouse?]; house with small barn, shed and fenced fields; and small house.

BACK OF THE POND

Property of William T. Matthews, Stephenville
(A 66-2)
1943-1944
Claim # 99S

BACK OF THE POND

Property of Nolan Russell, Stephenville
(A 66-21)
1943-1944
Claim # 133S

Side view of house with man at front door and clothesline.

BACK OF THE POND

Property of Norbert Russell, Stephenville
(A 66-22)
1944
Claim # 96S

House with garage and fence.

BACK OF THE POND

Property of Peter Russell, Stephenville
(A 66-23, A 66-24)
1943-1944
Claim # 126S

Two views: house; and two small sheds with fence in foreground.

BACK OF THE POND

Property of Stephen Russell, Stephenville
(A 66-25)
1942-1944
Claim # 40S

House near water.

Property of Thaddeus Russell, Stephenville
(A 66-26)
1943-1944
Claim #95S

Small store with garage-style doors on left side.

BACK OF THE POND

Property of Vincent Russell, Stephenville
(A 66-27)
1939-1942
Claim # 47S

BACK OF THE POND

Property of Vincent Russell, Stephenville
(A 66-28)
1943-1948
Claim # 120S

BACK OF THE POND

Property of William A. Sauer, Stephenville
(A 66-29)
1943-1946
Claim # 170S

Tar paper building.

BACK OF THE POND

Property of David A. Morgan, Stephenville
(A 66-3)
1943
Claim # 116S

Two small buildings used as house and general store.

Property of David Schumpf, Stephenville
(A 66-30)
1943-1946
Claim # 168S

Hay barn.

BACK OF THE POND

Property of Isaac Sheppard, Stephenville
(A 66-31, A 66-32)
1941-1946
Claim # 154S

Two views: small cabin; small house.

BACK OF THE POND

Property of Estate of Albert Simon, Stephenville
(A 66-33)
1938-1944
Claim # 149S

Two story house with ladder on side.

BACK OF THE POND

Property of Harold Simon, Stephenville
(A 66-34)
1943-1948
Claim # 150S

BACK OF THE POND

Property of John Simon, Stephenville
(A 66-35)
1942
Claim # 42S

BACK OF THE POND

Property of Albert Thomas, Stephenville
(A 66-36)
1943-1944
Claim # 160S

Hay barn.

BACK OF THE POND

Property of Elias Tuma, Stephenville
(A 66-37)
1943
Claim # 68S

Four commercial retail stores. Claim refers to a hardware and jewelry store.

BACK OF THE POND

Property of John Francis Turner, Stephenville
(A 66-38)
1942-1943
Claim # 97S

BACK OF THE POND

Property of George W. Wells, Stephenville
(A 66-39)
1943-1944
Claim # 108S

Second hand store with variety of bed frames in front. Sign over door: M. Eddy.

BACK OF THE POND

Property of McFatridge, Charles H., Stephenville
(A 66-4, A 66-5, A 66-6, A 66-7)
1941-1942
Claim # 100S

Four views: men working on building removed from level foundation; building partially on foundation; Harmon Café; and empty wooden foundation and floor.

File indicates building was used as a bunkhouse.

BACK OF THE POND

Property of Robert G. Wells, Stephenville
(A 66-40, A 66-41)
1943-1946
Claim # 156S

Two views: small house with large addition; and partially built house.

BACK OF THE POND

Property of Aiden J. White, Stephenville
(A 66-44)
1943-1946
Claim # 72S

Small tar-papered house.

BACK OF THE POND

Property of Albert White, Stephenville
(A 66-42, A 66-43)
1943
Claim # 169S

Two views: House with attached porch and wood shed; and old barn with missing wall.

BACK OF THE POND

Property of Alexander H. White, Stephenville
(A 66-45)
1943
Claim # 177S

Small house with baby's cradle on porch roof.

BACK OF THE POND

Property of Aloysius White, Stephenville
(A 66-46)
1941
Claim # 3S

House with fences.

Property of Aloysius White, Stephenville
(A 66-47, A 66-48)
1943
Claim # 148S

Two views of different small stores.

BACK OF THE POND

Property of Andrew H. White, Stephenville
(A 66-49)
1943-1944
Claim # 104S

Small house with outhouse.

BACK OF THE POND

Property of Bert White, Stephenville
(A 66-58)
1943-1944
Claim # 114S

BACK OF THE POND

Property of Cecilia White (Mrs. Remy White), Stephenville
(A 66-59)
1943-1944
Claim # 157S

BACK OF THE POND

Property of Charles A. White, Stephenville
(A 66-60)
1943-1944
Claim # 71S

Small house with various sheds and well house.

BACK OF THE POND

Property of Charles D. White, Stephenville
(A 66-61, A 66-62)
1942
Claim # 22S

Two views: large house with building and tower behind; and barn with cows and two-wheeled cart.

BACK OF THE POND

Property of Charles H. White, Stephenville
(A 66-63)
1943-1944
Claim # 105S

BACK OF THE POND

Property of Columbus White, Stephenville
(A 66-64, A 66-65)
1941
No claim number cited

Two views: house and two sheds; and barn.

BACK OF THE POND

Property of Columbus White, Stephenville
(A 66-66, A 66-67)
1943-1944
Claim # 122S

Two views: two-storied house; and partially completed two-storied house.

Property of Mrs. David White, Stephenville
(A 66-68, A 66-69)
1941
No claim number cited

Two views: house with small shed; and barn with fence.

BACK OF THE POND

Property of Euzeb White, Stephenville
(A 66-70, A 66-71, A 66-72)
1942
Claim # 23S

Three views: farm yard with small buildings, animal cage and various carts; large barn with wood-pile; and small house and store.

BACK OF THE POND

Property of Euzeb White, Stephenville
(A 66-73, A 66-74)
1943-1944
Claim # 73S

Two views: small store; and hay shed.

BACK OF THE POND

Property of Francis White, Stephenville
(A 66-75)
1941
No claim number cited

BACK OF THE POND

Property of Estate of Henry White, Stephenville
(A 66-76, A 66-77)
1942
Claim # 35S

Property of Herbert White, Stephenville
(A 66-78, A 66-79)
1941-1944
Claim # 102S

Two views: three door garage and wooded lot.

BACK OF THE POND

Property of Lawrence O'Gorman, Stephenville
(A 66-8)
1943-1944
Claim # 174S

BACK OF THE POND

Property of Hubert White, Stephenville
(A 66-80)
1942
Claim # 36S

Partially built house.

BACK OF THE POND

Property of James V. White, Stephenville
(A 66-81)
1941-1942
No claim number cited

BACK OF THE POND

Property of John A. White, Stephenville
(A 66-82)
1943-1944
Claim # 176S

BACK OF THE POND

Property of John White Jr., Stephenville
(A 66-84)
1942
Claim # 21S

BACK OF THE POND

Property of Joseph H. White, Stephenville
(A 66-85, A 66-86)
1943-1944
Claim # 107S

Two views: small house; and small shed.

BACK OF THE POND

Property of Mrs. Leo White, Stephenville
(A 66-87)
1941
No claim number cited

BACK OF THE POND

Property of Maurice White, Stephenville
(A 66-88)
1942
Claim # 24S

BACK OF THE POND

Property of O'Dallon White, Stephenville
(A 66-89, A 66-90, A 66-91)
1943-1946
Claim # 66S

View three different houses: large house in open field, large house with two wind chargers and woman at open well house, small house with tower for wind charger and wood pile and various household items in front.

BACK OF THE POND

Property of John O'Neill, Stephenville
(A 66-9)
1943-1944
Claim # 153S

House with fences.

BACK OF THE POND

Property of Estate of Oneseme White, Stephenville
(A 66-92)
1941-1943
Claim # 10S

Property of Patrick and Columbus White, Stephenville
(A 66-93, A 66-94)
1941
No claim number cited

Two views: two-storied house with shed; and small barn.

BACK OF THE POND

Property of Stephen White, Stephenville
(A 66-95)
1941
No claim number cited

House with barn and shed and fences. Three quilts hanging on fence.

BACK OF THE POND

Property of Stephen White, Stephenville
(A 66-96, A 66-97)
1941-1943
Claim # 113S

Two views: two houses with line of laundry; and large barn.

BACK OF THE POND

Property of Telesphore White, Stephenville
(A 66-98, A 66-99)
1941-1942
Claim # 7S

Two views: House with fence; and two barns.

BACK OF THE POND

A contentious issue arose when the construction of the bases began, and the Newfoundland workers were being paid the same wages as American and Canadian civilians. They got equal pay for equal work. The St. John's establishment realized that those rates, which were generally higher than those paid in Newfoundland, would entice the locals to the jobs on the bases, leaving industrial and service jobs strapped for workers. If paid more by the Americans, they could also foresee that their present workers would be looking for an increase in pay, to be on par with others or to be enticed into leaving. Rather than seeing the up side of increased wages for Newfoundland, the establishment saw it as a problem.

The bases had a variety of job openings in skilled and unskilled positions. Also, it must be remembered that, for the very first time, Newfoundlanders were being offered good "cash-paying" jobs, that our outport women could fill. Previously, there had been very few opportunities for women in the outports other than in the fishery.

The merchant political establishment took it upon themselves to lobby the Commission of Government to pay lower wages. The benefit of years of new wealth for the whole country was reduced as a result of this. To illustrate, the Newfoundland civilians, who worked on the base, had the letter L, for local, put in front of their name or pay scale. The Americans had the letter L omitted. Thus, the locals, classified as LGS, received x amount per hour, while the non-locals were classified as GS, receiving a higher wage per hour. To further demonstrate the bias of the merchant political establishment, other bases in Newfoundland, such as Gander, Argentia and Goose Bay were also negatively impacted. The pay scales in *all* installations were lowered for the locals, in the same way that they were in Stephenville.

In keeping with the same mindset, the merchant political establishment used its influence to control how the monies from the American Government would be spent. Using the generous amount of money given to them for the expropriation claims on the bases, they took over the job of compensating. They under-paid some and were fair only to those who would benefit them.

BACK OF THE POND

Back of the Pond Diorama "small scale replica" by William (Billy) White born in 1910 son of Caliste LeBlanc (born 1869) and Marguerite (Benoit) LeBlanc, Stephenville Crossing

Please note that these claims took place in the early 1940s, when there were few lines of communication between the west coast and the east coast of Newfoundland. On the west coast, the Acadians were isolated from the capital by language. That was not the case in St. John's or Argentia because they had counselors who understood their language and could arbitrate on their behalf. These counselors were local and accessible to them, which was very much to their advantage.

Here in Stephenville, the amount of legal advice was limited.

BACK OF THE POND

Initially, one would notice immediately a large discrepancy between how land was valued in the official documents, and how the land was undervalued in the Stephenville area.

In the case of Vincent Russell's claim, however, he got full payment for just 12.17 acres, and was paid much less for the remainder of his property.

> NAME: Vincent Russell
>
> Parcel No.
>
> 12.17 acres cultivated @ $250.00 = $ 3042.50
>
> 6.34 acres wooded @ $100.00 = $ 634.00
>
> 2.00 acres pasturage @ $150.00 = $ 300.00
>
> 1.00 acres marsh @ $ 40.00 = $ 40.00
>
> TOTAL = $4016.50

The remaining acreage, however, was no less valuable. His land provided lumber, fire wood, animal feed, wild fruit and flood control. In fact, even the percentage paid for the disturbance was twice as much on the Avalon as here on the west coast.

This is merely one example of an official correspondence regarding a requisitioned property, and the amounts paid for acreages of land.

The following, typed *verbatim* from official government documents, provides examples of some of the exchanges between members of the arbitration board and the claimants.

BACK OF THE POND

CLAIMANT 1

Vincent Russell (Lot #93, Claim #120S)

Q. Where do you live?

A. Stephenville (East)

Q. You received notice that your property was being taken over by the government?

A. Yes.

Q. How long has this property been in your possession?

A. 25 years.

Q. All buildings built the same time?

A. House, store-house and barn.

BACK OF THE POND

Q. Are these measurements approximately correct?

A. Yes.

Q. What do you value your house?

A. Not less than $4000

(Line 10) Q. How do you arrive at that figure?

A. Taking 30,000 feet of lumber, plane it, and take 3 months to build it. Three men at $15 a day. The chimney alone would cost $75. Glass and window boxes (14 sets); 2 boxes $30; 12 lbs. putty at 12¢; window frames $2.50 a set (14 sets).

Q. How many doors?

A. 9 at $10= $90; hinges $2.50 per door; nails $500 lbs. at 15¢ lb; foundation $300.

Q. Does that $300 include the digging?

A. Yes, everything.

Q. Where would you get the lumber?

A. We may get it here; I'm not sure. $60. We may have to pay extra for cartage. $6 a thousand from here to the station.

Q. What kind of roofing on the house?

A. Slate surface roofing. When I laid it on the roof first it was $2.25 a roll and I used 10 rolls. That was 25 years ago.

BACK OF THE POND

Q. How many rooms?

A. 9 rooms. 50 rolls of paper 40 and 50¢ a roll. 7 gallons of paint inside at $7 a gallon.; 4 gallons outside for one coat; 2 coats would be 8 gallons needed. I may be making a mistake on the inside, sometimes we paint over the sheathing paper.

Q. What would be the labor, painting inside and outside?

A. 12 days, 2 hands at $5 a day.

Q. What about your stairs?

A. $150

(Refer back to Line 10) Mr Baird: Q. Have you a concrete basement all around?

A. No.

Mr Baird: I alter the figure $300 to $100.

Q. Have you a fence around the house?

A. Yes.

Q. What kind of porch?

A. I am figuring the porch and all in that figure. The garage belongs to my son, Norbert Russell.

Q. Did you give him the land on which to build the garage?

A. Yes.

Q. How much land?

A. ½ an acre.

BACK OF THE POND

Q. He put up the garage himself?

A. Yes.

Q. Does the woodhouse belong to you?

A. Yes.

Q. What would it cost to build today?

A. There is a cellar underneath; would cost $500 today.

Q. How much lumber?

A. 1000 feet at the same price. Rough board, clapboard and sheathing outside. No sheathing inside. No windows in it.

Q. Barn. How is it constructed?

A. Same as the woodhouse; sheathing outside, clapboard, rough lumber.

Q. What foundation?

A. Just on shores.

Q. How much would it cost to paint?

A. I use lime on it.

Q. How much would it cost to build a barn like that?

A. Could not build less than $1800.

Q. How long would it take to build?

A. One month with 2 hands, that is as low as I could go.

Q. Toilet is 4 x 4 x 6. What would that cost to build?

A. $30

BACK OF THE POND

Q. Earth Cellar?

A. Outside cellar built out of timber costs $40. I have also a well 26 feet deep. Cannot build it less than $50.

Q. How much land?

A. 6.14 acres

Witness. It was signed to me by my father under Will.

Q. Cultivated?

A. 1 acre, not cultivated, and that is timberland. I used to grow 100 barrels potatoes; couple tons hay.

Q. How much do you pay for potatoes?

A. $2.10 sack

Q. How much for hay?

A. $20 delivered here.

Q. Fruit trees?

A. 31 fruit trees.

Q. What kind?

A. Apple and plum.

Mr. Baird: Q. What are they worth?

A. $10 each.

Q. How old?

A. Some 10 years, some less.

BACK OF THE POND

Q. What did you make off them?

A. They are just coming to maturity now.

Mr. Fox (cont.)

Q. What other crops?

A. Strawberries.

Q. How many gallons?

A. We got 30-40 gallons year. We got from 80¢ to $1 a gallon for them.

Q. Did you grow anything else?

A. Yes, turnips.

Q. How much turnips?

A. 200 lbs.; 1000 lbs. cabbage, 300-400 lbs. carrots

Q. What is the price of cabbage today?

A. 25¢ lb.

Q. Carrots?

A. 10¢ this year. I have nothing in the ground. We could not grow the hay this year. We are still occupying the house. Three in family.

Q. What do you value the cultivated land?

A. $250 an acre.

Mr. Bradshaw: The measurements of the land you gave us do not agree with the measurements on the plan. Where did you get the idea of 8 acres?

A. I always heard it was 8 acres. I am only making a guess.

BACK OF THE POND

CLAIMANT 2

Joseph F. Russell (Lot #94, Claim #59S)

House. garage, woodhouse, barn, toilet, cellar and well.

Q. What else is on your property?

A. Nothing else. Garage belongs to Norbert.

Q. You value your house at what?

A. $4000

Q. Earth cellar?

A. $40

Q. Well?

A. $50

Q. 6.14 acres of land?

A. $450 an acre. All cultivated, except 1 acre. I am taking off ½ acre each for my sons. Actual acreage 5.14 acres for myself, ½ acre for Norbert; ½ acre for Theodore.

Mr. Bradshaw: What do you think lumber costs landed on the job?

A. We cannot get it less than $75 a thousand, landed here.

BACK OF THE POND

Mr. Fox: How many panels of fencing have you?

A. 215 panels.

Q. What do you estimate that per panel?

A. $1 per panel.

I also forgot to mention my kitchen cabinet- built in.

Q. Did you include that in your estimate?

A. I estimate that at $50.

Q. Anything else?

A. Windows. 19 sets in house.

Q. At how much?

A. $2.50 set (5 extra windows - $12.50)

Mr. Bradshaw: In addition to the $40?

A. Yes, there are windows around my front door; 5 extra windows around the door.

Q. How much a window?

A. $25 for the whole lot. 14 rolls sheathing paper between the clapboard and the sheathing.

Q. When did your father die?

A. 13 years ago

Q. How did your father get the land?

A. He had a grant. Vincent Russell has the grant. Father had it first. He left it to Vincent.

BACK OF THE POND

Q. Are you Vincent Russell's brother?

A. Yes, father willed a piece to each of us. My brother holds the grant. I have had the land 38 years. My first house was burned.

Q. When was the house painted last?

A. 5 years ago. It was papered inside last year.

In the matter of the Defense (Acquisitioning of Land) regulations, 1940 and in the matter of the claim of Joseph Russell of Stephenville

Receipt and Indemnity

I, <u>Joseph Russell</u> of Stephenville in the Island of Nfld, hereby acknowledge to have received from the Govt. of Nfld, the sum of $220.00, and I hereby accept the said sum as full payment and compensation for the purchase price of all land, buildings and other property belonging to me and requisitioned and possessed by the Crown, under the provisions of the above mentioned regulations (the said land being delineated and shown on the official plan of the Dept. of Public Works and thereon marked as lot #A66, 19, 20, and in full satisfaction of all loss and damage whatsoever suffered by me, by reason of such requisitioning and possession.

And I do hereby undertake and agree that I will, at all times, hereafter indemnify and keep indemnified the Govt. of Nfld. against the said purchase price and compensation as aforesaid, and from all actions, proceedings, claims, and demands, by any person or persons in respect of the said land, buildings and property above mentioned, which may be made by reason of any alleged defect or want of title in me to the same or of any other act or thing permitted or done by the Govt. of Nfld, its servants or agents in respect of the said property.

As with my hand this 26th day of Sept. 1941.

Signed by the said Joseph Russell in the presence of <u>W. L. Whelan</u>

BACK OF THE POND

CLAIMANT 3

Exchange between another Vincent Russell and members of the arbitration board.

Q. How many acres of land have you?

A. 32 acres.

Mr. Robinson: 23.4 is what we show; just one piece of land.

Mr. Whelan: He says the grant from Francis Russell was 72 acres.

Q. I believe the base has already taken 10 acres?

A. Yes

Joseph F. Russell - 6 acres

Fred Gabriel - 6 acres

Vincent Russell, Norbert Russell - 6 acres

Peter Russell - 6½ acres

July 22, 1943

That is 34½ acres altogether.

Chairman: Did you ever have the land measured?

A. 5 years ago. I never measured what I got left.

Q. There is quite a discrepancy in the acreage?

A. It runs up to Noel's Pond. I have 10 chains on one side.

Mr. Higgins: Is it possible that others have taken more than their share?

Mr. Whelan: I was acting for Peter Russell and he says he has 10 acres.

BACK OF THE POND

Mr. Higgins: Our experience is that the old surveys were bad; land was overlapping.

Q. Mr. Whelan: How much land is cleared?

A. About 7 acres.

Q. The rest is timberland?

A. Yes, timber and wood.

Mr. Higgins: Is the cleared land cultivated?

A. Yes.

Q. Mr. Whelan: On this cleared land you have a dwelling house and some other buildings?

A. Yes.

Q. How old is the house?

A. 26 years old.

Measurements are agreed upon.

Q. What is the replacement value?

A. $3,726.50

Q. Woodhouse is a store, including cellar under it, you value it at $210?

A. Yes.

Q. Barn? (Measurements agreed)

Q. You have a shed on the farm?

A. Yes 17 x 12 x 8

BACK OF THE POND

Q. When did you build that?

A. Last fall in December.

Q. You have a value of $1340.44 for the barn and the shed.

Shed $180.00

Barn $1160.44

$1340.44

Q. Earth Cellar?

A. Yes, 8 ft. h.

Mr. Robinson: The pit under the ground not taken in.

Q. What do you value it?

A. $75

Q. You have a well?

A. 12 ft. deep value $90.

Q. Toilet (outdoor)?

A. $25

Q. In 1942, you built an addition to the barn to house your cattle? You had a permit for building?

A. Yes.

Q. You have some fruit trees?

A. 9 fruit trees; all plum.

BACK OF THE POND

Q. How old?

A. About 10 years old.

Q. All bearing fruit?

A. Yes.

Q. What do you value them?

A. $10 each = $90

Q. You have an item here "bearing 7 gallons each or $1 per gallon or $63?

A. Yes.

Q. If you can get them, you will not have any charge?

A. No.

Q. In your statement you have 240 panels of fence at $1 per panel?

A. Yes.

Q. Is there anything else?

A. I got my hay. I had to put the cattle in the hayfield. Loss of hay 7 tons. I put the cattle in the field and could not get the hay-crop. I could not leave them loose. I had no other place to put them. They would not allow me to put them out.

Chairman: Do you usually leave them loose?

Mr. Higgins: They could not let them roam over private property such as the base is. What did the other people do?

A. I suppose they got pasture. I had not any pasture.

BACK OF THE POND

Mr. Whelan: You could not have your cattle at large?

A. No they used to go up on the base.

Chairman: Where did they graze last year?

Mr. Whelan: He had the place below. That was taken.

Mr. Higgins. He was paid for that.

Mr. Whelan: At what do you value the hay?

A. At $40 a ton.

Q. Did you get any warning or did anyone tell you to keep the cattle off the base?

A. Yes, the man at the booth.

Mr. Higgins: They could seize his cattle if it went in there. He has no business to have cattle on private property.

Mr. Whelan: Any other claim?

A. I had 2 barrels potatoes planted.

Q. What is the estimated yield?

A. 60 barrels.

Q. What do you value that?

A. $8 a barrel.

Q. If you are not allowed to dig, you are claiming value of those potatoes?

A. Yes.

BACK OF THE POND

Q. Anything else?

A. I have one acre raspberries.

Q. How many gallons?

A. 1000 gallons.

Q. Did you actually pick them?

A. Yes, I can pick 2000.

"Chairman reminds witness, he is under oath."

Q. Did you ever pick 1000 gallons?

A. I never wanted them.

Mr. Higgins: Did you ever sell raspberries?

A. Yes, we sell them all summer.

Q. Did you sell many?

A. 100 or 150 gallons at 50¢ a gallon.

Q. How much do you use yourself?

A. 60 or 70 gallons.

Q. Do you know how much jam that makes or how much sugar?

A. No.

BACK OF THE POND

CLAIMANT 4

Stephenville
March 31, 1941
Sir Wilfred Woods
Dept. of Public Utilities
St. John's

Herewith submitted is a statement of property owned by me at Stephenville, and now to be transferred to the United States government defenses here, with valuation of same.

1 dwelling house size 22 ft. by 25 ft. high, 15 ft. value $1200 (twelve hundred dollars)

1 barn size 15 ft. by 25 ft. height 10 ft., value $125 (one hundred and twenty-five dollars)

Twenty-one acres of land, valued at $125 (one hundred twenty-five dollars per acre),

1 well—size 3 ft. square, depth 14 ft, value $20 (twenty dollars).

In my opinion, the sum of $35 (thirty-five dollars) should be allowed for all the inconveniences and sacrifice that the members of my family will be obliged to undergo during the period of my rehabilitation.

If I receive payment in full at once, I am prepared to vacate the property now, on the base, without further delay.

Yours truly,

Harold Russell

BACK OF THE POND

The arbitration board was very meticulous in its proceedings concerning evaluations of properties. But in the case of Mr. Russell, someone has miscalculated his 10% disturbance claim at $35.00 instead of $397.00 on property that totaled $3970.00.

The onus should have been on the educated, honorable board members to use the same scrutiny to compensate the farmers fairly, in what could have been their finest hours.

Harold Russell MG/GN #413   Do #20   F M G/4451/33   Parcel #74

Framed 2 storey house 22ft. x 25ft.8 in x 17 ft. 2 in. rise for roof	$2431.00
Wood house 10 ft.6 in. x 12 ft.6 in. x 7 ft. 2 in. rise for roof	$74.00
Barn (1 storey) 15 ft. 6 in. x 15 ft.3 in. x 9 ft. 6 in.- 1 ft. 6 in. rise for roof	$192.00
Lean to, shed to barn, attach 10 ft. x 7ft. x 7 ft.	$39.00
Toilet 6 ft. x 6 ft. x 6 ft. 6 in.	$10.00
Wall covered in wood 4 ft. x 4 ft. x 3ft. 6in.	$10.00

Total cost $2756.00

Harold Russell File   MG/GN #413   70   File   4451/33

1.05 cultivated acres at $250.00 = 762.50

11.36 wooded acres at $100.00 = 1136.00

Acreage 14.41 = 1898.50

Buildings = 2756.00

Total = 4659.50

Further investigation reveals even greater inequalities, as the arbitration board failed to appreciate the monumental loss, of not only their property and homes, but also of their farming way of life.

BACK OF THE POND

The following is another example of just how Americans viewed the Bay St. George area. It is an original document written by an American teacher and wife of an American officer, who wrote of her experiences after she came to Harmon Field in the summer of 1953. I received this information, courtesy of the Stephenville Cultural Destination Committee.

THE SO-CALLED ARCTIC

February 8, 1958

My family, all my friends and even I, shivered, rechecked my luggage for woolen underwear, scarves, mittens, and regretted for the thousandth time that the Alabama stores did not have mukluks, snow-pacs and ski suits for me and the kids.

When they all told me goodbye on my departure to join my husband in Stephenville, Newfoundland, where he was serving a recall to service for three years, we were all sure that Newfoundland was just a hop, skip and jump from the North Pole. What a surprise I had when the children and I fully prepared to slide off the plane onto the ice, stepped out into July sunshine and mud, mud, mud.

Of course, it isn't all mud now. The mud has been pushed out with the sheep and cows that used to help me shop on Main Street. Stephenville then was of 3,000 population, no paved streets, street lights nor water and sewage; an excellent replica of a town in a western movie back home. My husband had used the only medium possible to get us with him. He had gotten permission to construct the first trailer park in Newfoundland. I wound up with a 40 ft. trailer and 45 trailer neighbors, only two blocks from the base.

Thanks to Dr. Lois Ackerley's often repeated advice "Girls, use your ingenuity," my gentle persuasion caused my husband to construct a house around our trailer, 800 sq. ft. in size and, with Sears' order house via A.P.O., it is decorated to accommodate 12 people. However, we and our three children find it spacious.

BACK OF THE POND

Stephenville today (1958) has over 8,000 population, a paved main street, street lights, a modern water and sewage installation, telephone service, department stores, groceterias and a FIVE AND DIME! A miraculous advancement; we feel a new frontier. By 1955, we recognized this face and my husband resigned his commission and we returned to Newfoundland in 1956 as Canadian Immigrants, not having to give up our citizenship in the U.S. though, opened Newfoundland's first Laundromat, increased the park to 96 units, including some with furnished accommodations for vacationers and sportsmen to our new-found-land.

Newfoundland has the greatest hunting and fishing in the world: salmon, trout, cod, flounder, lobster, seal, black bear, moose, caribou and duck, all within a twenty-five mile range of Stephenville. Trans-Canada Air Lines opened a new terminal within two blocks of our home last year. The Canadian National Railway runs a ferry service to and from North Sydney, Nova Scotia, to Port aux Basques, which is 200 miles one way. In addition, it also runs a rail service to and from Port aux Basques to Stephenville Crossing, which takes 5 hours and is just 11 miles from where we live, here in Stephenville. The highway will be complete all through the island this summer, to St. John's on the eastern coast.

There is such bog here, sometimes 20 feet or more deep, that it took the Army Engineers (my husband's unit) four years to construct eleven miles of road to connect the base here with the Trans-Canada Highway. You will find lakes on top of mountains. It will snow and rain, yet within 24 hours you will see dust on the roads. The winters are really nice here. The temperature rarely drops to zero, usually stays around 15-25 degrees above, and is a dry cold, that the children easily adjust to and seldom are sick. Do they ever love the snow with the sledding, skating and ice hockey that are a part of winter here!

We have two boys and a daughter. Wayne is 7 and a 2nd grader, Cris is 5 and in kindergarten and our female blonde, Biki, is 4 now and our good relations gal in this foreign country. This is a French-speaking section but so far we still manage to speak English, even with a southern accent. Claxton and I have more of an accent that sounds southern than do the children. Our foods have recipes on the packages in both languages. The average family here is from 8 to 12 children and is predominately Catholic, with a small Amalgamated school in town.

I teach 6th grade at the Base School. This is my 4th year teaching, having taught Public School Music the first 2 years. Corrie Posey Williams, graduate '54 Alabama College, teaches 4th grade here this year and will be here for a 3 year tour. Small world!

I have a full-time local girl that lives in and does the domestic work. Domestic help is still plentiful here in this section and I find them particularly good with the children. We have 650 school children on the base and it is increasing all the time. We have 28 teachers in our system and I have 35 6th graders. My husband, an engineer, pursues his business ventures and is employed by J. A. Jones Construction Company, of North Carolina, in the construction of additional facilities on the base. We are enjoying our dual role of American citizens on Harmon Field and Canadian immigrants in Stephenville. Of course, we get in some very peculiar situations when the question comes up, as to where one stops and the other begins. Claxton serves his two weeks reserve training on this base each year.

Both our families have visited us twice, one time driving through to Nova Scotia and over by boat and the other time flying – only seven hours from Boston. The ferry boat ride from North Sydney, Nova Scotia, is only 12 hours across and brings you to the tip of the island, 70 miles away. You can then drive here or take a five hour train trip that will bring you here. We would love to have any of you visit our so-called arctic country.

The largest paper mill in the world is at Corner Brook, only 60 miles away. Mining, fishing, and sealing are large industries too. Farming sections produce some fabulous vegetables: 25 lb. heads of cabbage, 2 ft. long carrots, Irish potatoes weighing 6 lbs. and strawberries as large as small peaches. Do I ever appreciate our deep freeze! The natives store theirs in root cellars as all root vegetables are grown here.

The country-side is a majestic continuity of nature's grandeur, miles and miles of thousands of lakes, teeming with fish, woodlands filled with wildlife, and in the fall with the first frost, millions of acres of the most brilliant red marsh and bog land flowers and multi-hued leaves. Throughout it all the native spruce and fir stay green all year round, looking like Christmas every day. The people are hard-working, God-fearing and cooperative. Newfoundland has come a long way since its Confederation with Canada as the 10th Province and we feel will go a lot further much faster in the next few years.

Thanks to the writer, Mrs. Claxton Ray (née Gay Cotney).

To quote Misty MacDonald and Heather Thistle in their 1998 article: "Stephenville Village was actually established because of poverty and strife existing in Nova Scotia, and the excellent fishing grounds and farm land that this community had to offer. Strangely enough, not many people know a lot of details about this era. It is almost like a lost memory which has been tucked away, even though it is a major part of Stephenville's history." [32]

---

[32] http://www.heritage.nf.ca/articles/society/acadian-village.php

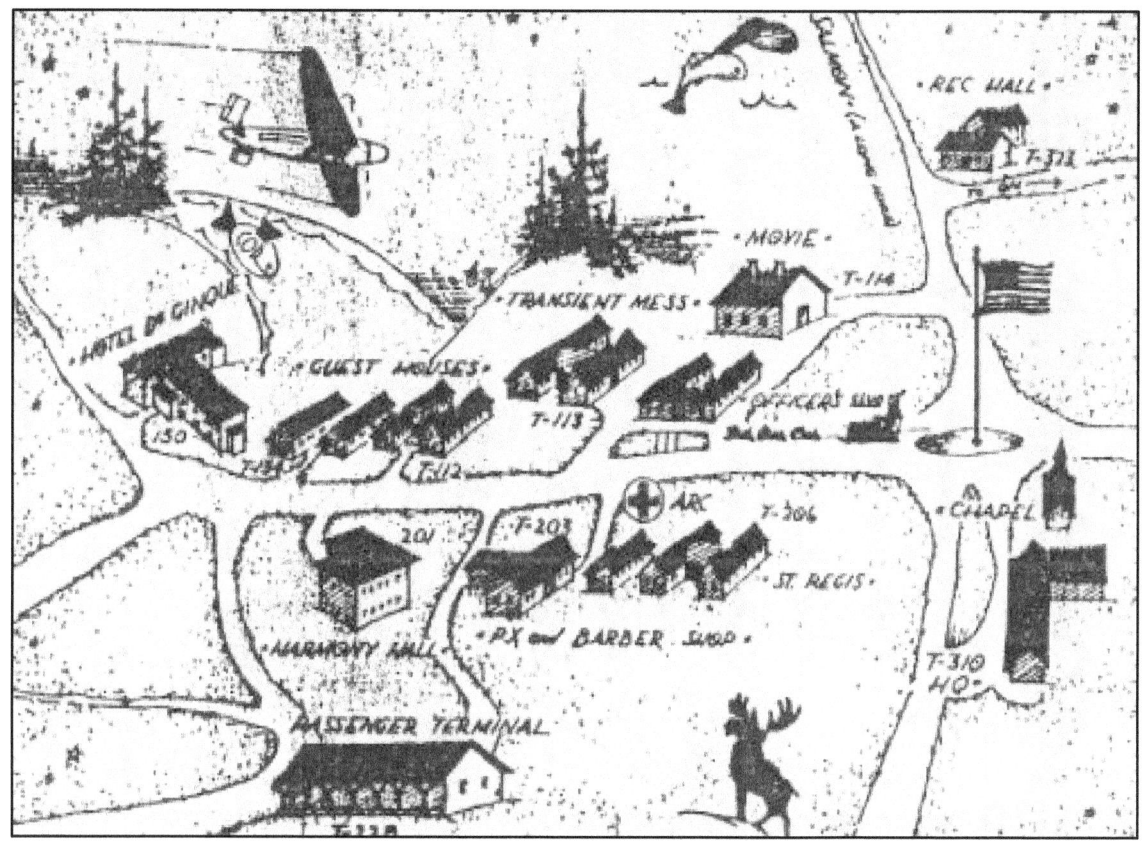
Sketch of Main Buildings on Ernest Harmon Air Force Base (closed in 1966)

Harmon Field Flyer compliments of Peggy Gale-Bennett

TO HARMON FIELD

THE place Frank Cipriani of the Chicago Tribune calls "The Switching Yard" of the Atlantic, and that Watson Davis of Science Service called "A little bit of U.S.A., we newly-found".

OUR MISSION here, is the mission of the host, and our business is to make your visit as pleasant and comfortable as our facilities permit.

Your stay with us may be for minutes, hours or days! It all depends on that weather man. But while you are with us, all our facilities for Amusement, Recreation and Stimulation, are at your disposal. Details are given

Harmon Field Flyer compliments of Peggy Gale-Bennett

without elevators . . . beds that are great for sack time . . . to
one dollar, with towels included. The Renaissance Room is recomm
breakfast, lunch and dinner. Hours 0700 to 2300.

BEDS: Officers: Harmony Hotel, Officers' Club, T-134, T-206.
Enlisted Men: Building T-112.

POST EXCHANGE: T-203, near the Harmony Hotel.

RECREATION—

MOVIES: The latest. You'll be surprised. Times 1430, 1830, 20
pine seats.

POOL: Two tables in the Officers' Club, several in Recreation H

OFFICERS' CLUB: Across from Transient Mess. Make yourself a
the Lounge, which is complete with radio, old magazines and n
chess and checkers. WE DO NOT GAMBLE IN OUR LOUNG

BOWLING: Four alleys in the Recreation Hall.

PING PONG: Officers' Club and Recreation Hall.

CULTURE AND THE ARTS: Found in the Post Library, direc
from the Flag Pole.

STIMULATION—

OFFICERS: The Stephenville "21" Club, at the far end of the
the Officers' Club. Popular after 1700.

NON-COMS: Non-Commissioned Officers' Club, T-131, at the
Bigger and better quarters under construction.

PRIVATES: The Canteen in the Post Exchange.

Enjoy yourselves, while here. Have a good trip and drop in again
we will still be here, no doubt!

Harmon Field Flyer compliments of Peggy Gale-Bennett

BACK OF THE POND

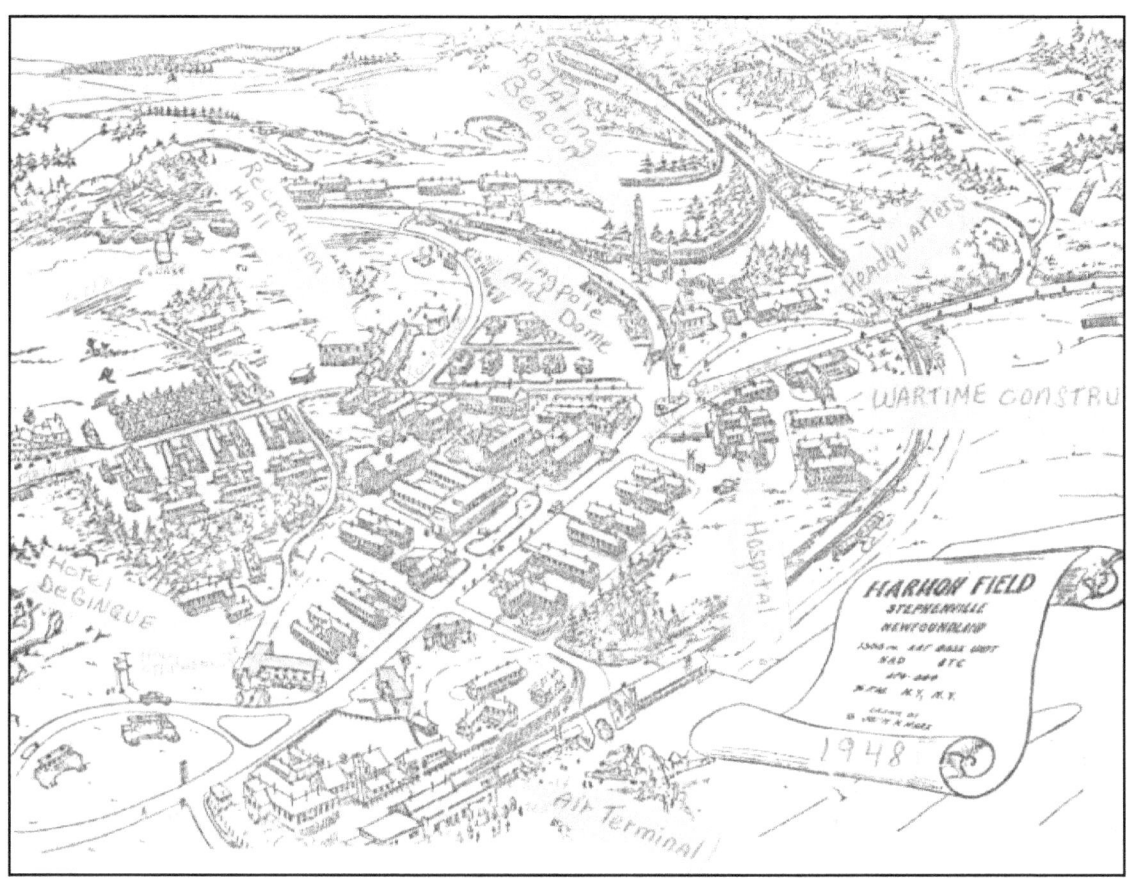

Harmon Field (Stephenville, Newfoundland) sketch drawn by T/S John N. Marx

Ron Vigneault and Theresa Penney (1961)

This photograph represents just one of thousands of marriages of American Servicemen to Newfoundland girls. Theresa is originally from Port au Port West, Aguathuna, and is the daughter of John Penney and Margaret O'Gorman.

Acknowledgments

I can honestly say that this document is a true example of the whole being the sum of its parts.

Firstly, I must thank my brother, Albert Benoit, for patiently listening to my first draft, at least half of which went into the garbage.

Secondly, I want to thank my friend, Beverly Harvey, for suffering through those long days and nights in our campers, or by the outdoor fire (I'm joking, of course). I don't think either of us was meant to live in a house; we enjoy the outdoors too much. On a more serious note, though, thanks Bev for being my critic for pages and pages of writing that I either threw away or got the final approval for. If it piqued your interest when I read it, it lived to see another day; if it was boring, it was either replaced or thrown out.

Thirdly, I want to thank Bill Pilgrim for endless hours, days, weeks, even months, of editing, from the introduction to the end of the book. It was a blast, and I enjoyed every minute of it; in doing so, I found a true friend.

Finally, when I thought all was lost, Ursula Schumph helped iron out all the wrinkles and molded all the pieces together, with illustrations and expertise, until she helped create the first edition of my book.

In addition, I also wish to thank many people, who helped me along the way, including: Aiden Young, Andrew Benoit, the family of the late Austin White (LeBlanc), Bay St. George Genealogical Society, Bill Penney, Bill Pike, Brian and Bradley Russell, Carleen Doucette, the family of the late Gerry Formanger, Janice Clarke (Port au Port East Library), Jena Archer, Jonathan Duffy, Judy (née Sheppard) Doucette, Kevin MacDonald, Kindale Library Staff, Lillian Retieffe, Linda Collier, Mary O'Quinn, Melinda Campbell, Mercedes Stevenson, Peggy Gale-Bennett, Regional Museum of Art and History, Robert Laite, Royal Canadian Legion Branch 35, Stephanie Gale,

BACK OF THE POND

Stephenville Cultural Destination Committee, Stephenville Historical Society Incorporated, Terry and Ann Penney, Tracy Hall, Willie and Audrey McNeil. A sincere thank you to all, no more to one than the other.

The image on the cover of this revised <u>Back of the Pond</u> edition was located on the Pixabay website. [33] The moment that I saw this picture, I knew that it was *the one* I had been looking for. I wish to extend my thanks to Hermann Schmider [34] for this breathtaking image.

Many thanks to Michele Doucette (Editor) and Kent Hesselbein (Graphic Design Artist responsible for cover design and photo restoration) of St. Clair Publications for assisting with this revised edition.

My wish is that you, the reader, have grasped every concept that I've tried meticulously to convey. If successful in doing so, then you will have enjoyed reading it, as much as I have enjoyed writing it.

---

[33] https://pixabay.com/en/lake-constance-sheep-pasture-sheep-1597503/
[34] https://pixabay.com/en/users/hschmider-3108740/

Bibliography

Allderdice Syndrome

Allderdice Syndrome is characterized in offspring with multiple congenital abnormalities, low birth weight, hand and facial abnormalities and psychomotor dysfunction. Also called Sandy Point Syndrome, Allderdice Syndrome is a genetic syndrome local to the people of Sandy Point, Newfoundland. It was discovered by Dr. Penny Allderdice in 1975.

Allderdice Syndrome [35]

Chromosome 3 Duplication, by P.W. Allderdice, N. Browse and Dr. P. Murphy, Faculty of Medicine at Memorial University of Newfoundland, pages 699-718, pictures page 711. [36]

Twisted Roots: Inversion 3 Chromosome (Canadian Broadcasting Corporation 1980) VHS Video [37]

American Occupation of Stephenville

Stephenville was inside the largest area specified in the 1940 land-lease agreement between the United States and Great Britain: 1859 acres of land in the northeast end of St. George's Bay. Harmon Field became the largest U.S. air force base outside the continental U.S. and a major refueling stop for aircraft en route to Europe. Construction began in 1941, with the creation of a support camp, where more than 1500 men from the surrounding area soon found work as tinsmiths, sheet metal workers, construction laborers, carpenters, etc. The population increased to over 7000 virtually overnight. The scope of the impact upon Stephenville was immense.

---

[35] https://prezi.com/t2k_nitvqcwq/allderdice-syndrome/
[36] https://www.ncbi.nlm.nih.gov/pmc/articles/PMC1762887/pdf/ajhg00439-0003.pdf
[37] http://www.worldcat.org/title/twisted-roots-inversion-3-chromosome/oclc/456478505

Higgins, Jenny. (2006) "Harmon Field, Stephenville." [38]

Harmon Field Stephenville Newfoundland Sketch Drawn by T/S John N. Mark

High, Steven. "From Outport to Base: The American Occupation of Stephenville, 1940-1945." *Newfoundland Studies* 18.1 (2002): 84-113. [39]

MacDonald, Misty, and Thistle, Heather. (1998) "Acadian Village." *Stephenville Integrated High School Project.* [40][41]

Maritime History Archive Public Photo Catalogue (photo of Aerial view of Ernest Harmon Air Force Base runways, Stephenville, Newfoundland circa 1942, page 122) [42]

Stephenville: From a French Farming Village into a Flourishing American Air Base blog article (2016) by Larry Dohey [43]

In order to build the air base the properties of local residents were expropriated by the Newfoundland Department of Public Utilities, Commission of Government, to provide sites for American military bases and installations under the Leased Lands Agreement and American Bases Act (1941).

The process of expropriation was documented and is now available at The Rooms Provincial Archives.

This new online collection consists of 265 photographs (black and white) relating to claims for remuneration for expropriated property in the community of Stephenville.

---

[38] http://www.heritage.nf.ca/articles/politics/stephenville-base.php
[39] https://spectrum.library.concordia.ca/976909/1/stephenville_article.pdf
[40] http://www.heritage.nf.ca/articles/society/acadian-village.php
[41] http://www.heritage.nf.ca/articles/society/stephenville-school-table-contents.php
[42] https://www.mun.ca/mha/pviewphoto/Record_ID/10468
[43] http://archivalmoments.ca/2016/11/stephenville-from-a-french-farming-village-into-a-flourishing-american-air-base/

BACK OF THE POND

The images illustrate houses, fences, shops, sheds, farms, farm animals, vehicles, buildings, and household items as per the recommended archival collection as per Department of Public Works Newfoundland Board of Arbitration records Expropriations claims: Photographs: GN 4.3, Series (Stephenville). [44]

Stephenville Integrated High School Project (1998)[45]

USAAF ~ USAF Bases FB Group [46] shares the following post (including the picture above) by Howard Spicer. Ernest Harmon Air Force Base is a former United States Air Force base located in Stephenville, Newfoundland and Labrador. The base was built by the United States Army Air Forces in 1941 under the Destroyers for Bases Agreement with the United Kingdom.

---

[44] http://gencat.eloquent-systems.com/therooms_permalink.html?key=38234
[45] http://www.heritage.nf.ca/articles/society/stephenville-school-table-contents.php
[46] https://www.facebook.com/groups/497269393757806/permalink/975862335898507/

From its establishment in 1941 until March 31, 1949, the base was located in the Dominion of Newfoundland. On March 31, 1949, the Dominion of Newfoundland was admitted to Canadian Confederation and became the 10th province of Canada. The agreement enabling the base's existence from 1941 until closure in 1966 enabled it to function as a de facto enclave of United States territory within, first the Dominion of Newfoundland and later Canada, making United States military personnel stationed at the base subject to the Uniform Code of Military Justice.

Following its closure in 1966, the base property was relinquished by the Government of the United States to the Government of Canada, under the terms of the original deal. The Government of Canada subsequently transferred the base property to the Government of Newfoundland and Labrador, which established the Harmon Corporation to oversee the disposition and use of the base property and facilities.

The airfield is now operated as Stephenville International Airport while many of the base's support buildings and housing have been incorporated into the town of Stephenville.

Bay St. George area (west coast of Newfoundland)

A Pioneer History of St. George's Diocese (1948) by Rev. Michael Brosnan, B.A., P.P. [47]

Dictionary of Canadian Biography: Bélanger, Alexis [48]

Franco-Newfoundlander [49]

The Early Settlers in the Codroy Valley [50]

---

[47] http://ngb.chebucto.org/Articles/pioneer-hist.shtml
[48] http://www.biographi.ca/en/bio/belanger_alexis_9E.html
[49] https://en.wikipedia.org/wiki/Franco-Newfoundlander
[50] http://www.rootsweb.ancestry.com/~cannf/wcod_jhbruce.htm

The History of Stephenville, Newfoundland [51]

West Coast Acadian Francophones [52]

West Coast: Early History [53]

Eric Cobham and Maria Lindsey

Eric Cobham (from Poole, England) and his wife, Maria Lindsey (from Plymouth, England) practiced piracy in the Gulf of St. Lawrence from their base on Sandy Point, Bay St. George (south-west coast of Newfoundland) for the better part of twenty years (1720-1740).

Archaeology in Newfoundland and Labrador 2006 [54]

Dalby, Paul. (January 9, 2016) "Canada's Pirate Queen: Pirate Maria Lindsey Cobham sent waves of fear through sailors in 1700s Canada." [55]

Eric Cobham and Maria Lindsey [56]

History Professor to Rebuff Story of Pirate Eric Cobham [57]

Genealogy Related

Acadiensis: Journal of The History of the Atlantic Region [58]

Bay St. George Genealogical Society [59]

___

[51] http://lc.wnlsd.ca/~judy.ldunphy/FOV1-00025091/FOV1-00029C78/S016B363D.1/History%20of%20Stephenville%20.pdf
[52] http://www.heritage.nf.ca/articles/society/west-coast-acadians.php
[53] http://www.rootsweb.ancestry.com/~cannf/wcboi_belanger.htm
[54] http://www.tcii.gov.nl.ca/pao/newsletters/pdf/Vol5-2007.pdf
[55] http://www.canadashistory.ca/Explore/Women/Canada-s-Pirate-Queen
[56] http://piracyinmediterranean.blogspot.ca/2009/12/eric-cobham-and-maria-lindsey_602.html
[57] http://www.thewesternstar.com/living/history-professor-to-rebuff-story-of-pirate-eric-cobham-141509/
[58] https://journals.lib.unb.ca/index.php/Acadiensis/
[59] http://www.bsggs.ca/

Newfoundland and Labrador Gen Web [60]

Newfoundland's Grand Banks Genealogy Site: District Menus [61]

Père Charles Aucoin Genealogy Centre (Chéticamp, Nova Scotia) [62]

HMS Hood

MacDonald, Kevin. "HMS Hood." Written for Grade 8 class in Stephenville, NL.

Introduction of Moose to Newfoundland

Bartibog, Mirimichi, New Brunswick, Canada: The Story of the Origin of the first Moose in Howley, Newfoundland [63]

Byrne, Allan. (2012) *The Introduction of Moose to the Island of Newfoundland* research paper. [64]

Moose are not native to Newfoundland? [65]

Newfoundland Dictionary

The Dictionary of Newfoundland English, first published in 1982 to regional, national and international acclaim, is a historical dictionary that gives the pronunciations and definitions for words that the editors have called "Newfoundland English." The varieties of English spoken in Newfoundland date back four centuries, mainly to the early seventeenth century migratory English fishermen of Cornwall, Devon, Dorset and Somerset, and to the seventeenth to the nineteenth century immigrants chiefly from south-eastern Ireland.

---

[60] http://www.rootsweb.ancestry.com/~cannf/
[61] http://ngb.chebucto.org/Districts/index.shtml
[62] https://www.lestroispignons.com/pere-charles-aucoin-genealogy-centre/
[63] http://www.howleynewfoundland.com/history.htm
[64] http://www.seethesites.ca/media/48059/introduction%20of%20moose.pdf
[65] http://archivalmoments.ca/2015/04/moose-are-not-native-to-newfoundland/

Culled from a vast reading of books, newspapers and magazines, this book is the most sustained reading ever undertaken of the written words of this province. The dictionary gives not only the meaning of words, but also presents each word with its variant spellings; moreover, each definition is succeeded by an all-important quotation of usage which illustrates the typical context in which word is used.

This well-researched, impressive work of scholarship illustrates how words and phrases have evolved and are used in everyday speech and writing in a specific geographical area.

The Dictionary of Newfoundland English is one of the most important, comprehensive and thorough works dealing with Newfoundland. This entertaining and delightful book presents a panoramic view of the social, cultural and natural history, as well as the geography and economics, of the quintessential lifestyle of one of Canada's oldest European-settled areas.

Dictionary of Newfoundland English edited by G. M. Story, W. J. Kirwin and J. D. A. Widdowson [66] [67]

Newfoundland Mi'kmaq

Hopper, Tristan. "*Extinction of Newfoundland's Lost People is a Myth, First Nations Chief Says.*" National Post article dated April 18, 2013. [68]

Martijn, Charles A. (2003) Early Mikmaq Presence in Southern Newfoundland: An Ethnohistorical Perspective. Newfoundland and Labrador Studies, Volume 19, Number 1: The New Early Modern Newfoundland, Part 2. [69]

---

[66] http://www.heritage.nf.ca/dictionary/a-z-index.php
[67] http://www.heritage.nf.ca/dictionary/
[68] http://nationalpost.com/news/canada/local-post
[69] https://journals.lib.unb.ca/index.php/NFLDS/article/view/141/238

BACK OF THE POND

Parrill, Erika. (2012) *We Always Did Fish The Eels: Perceptions of the Qalipu Mi'kmaq First Nation Band Members' Ecological Impacts in the American Eel Fisheries of Western Newfoundland* research paper. [70]

Seal Rocks: First Treaty Based (1804) Permanent Settlement of Mi'kmaq on the Island of Newfoundland. [71]

St. George's Bay Mi'kmaq [72]

The History of the Newfoundland Mi'kmaq [73]

There is an image of Molly Miuse (the name was originally Mius and is now spelled Meuse and Muse as well) from Annapolis Royal, Nova Scotia, that belongs to the Mi'kmaq Portraits Collection. [74] This may be the earliest portrait of a Mi'kmaq by a photographic process. It is further denoted that Molly *lived to a great age and was so much respected by her white neigbors that they erected a tombstone to her memory.*

Answer to the riddle on page 26 is "a Splinter."

---

[70] http://ruralresilience.ca/wp-content/uploads/2013/10/Parrill-WeAlwaysDidFishtheEels.pdf
[71] http://www.sgibnl.ca/traditional-sites-newfoundland-seal-rocks/
[72] http://www.benoitfirstnation.ca/village.html
[73] http://www.heritage.nf.ca/articles/aboriginal/mikmaq-history.php
[74] http://novascotia.ca/museum/mikmaq/?section=image&page=&id=116&period=1850&region=

BACK OF THE POND

Family Picture 2005 (missing Agnita (Mom) who died in 1972)
4 Boys L – R: Vernon, Albert, Tommy, Larry
Resting position: Paddy Benoit (Dad)
4 Girls L – R: Linda, Ann, Nina, Mercedes

BACK OF THE POND

Family Picture of Author
Back Row L – R: Daughter, Laura; son, Bobby; Daughter, Dawn
Front L – R: Husband, Bill; Mercedes

About the Author

Mercedes Benoit-Penney was born, raised and educated in Stephenville. She graduated with a Bachelor of Arts/Education Degree from Memorial University. As a teacher and mother, she advocated for educational standards in the local school system and wrote editorials for newspapers and magazines.

Mercedes began writing during her school years for therapeutic reasons, which developed into a passion in later years to record the ancestry of her Acadian background. She is now retired and devoting more time to her music as well as researching the diverse culture of the area.

Notes

As with all written works of historical, geographical and/or genealogical importance, record keeping is important. These pages are here for you to use in this manner.

BACK OF THE POND

BACK OF THE POND

BACK OF THE POND